English Reading and Comprehension

Teacher's Book

Ian Gordon

MACMILLAN

Macmillan Education
Between Towns Road, Oxford OX4 3PP
A division of Macmillan Publishers Limited
Companies and representatives throughout the world

ISBN 140502819 X

First published 2002, this edition published 2003.

Designed by eMC Design
Cover design by Stafford & Stafford

Printed and bound by Zamzam Presses, Egypt

2007 2006 2005 2004 2003
10 9 8 7 6 5 4 3 2 1

Introduction

1: Aims

The three books in the Macmillan *English Reading and Comprehension* series have been designed to improve the comprehension and communication skills of students of English. It is assumed that these students will have already learnt the fundamental rules of English grammar and will also have acquired a basic vocabulary. These books are intended to extend that vocabulary and students' reading skills, and to address some of the most common problems students at this stage need to confront to understand different types of writing. The passages also provide the stimulus for short, related writing assignments.

2: The texts

A wide variety of writing styles has been chosen: informative, narrative, explanatory and persuasive. A similarly wide range of sources has been exploited, for example encyclopaedia and reference book entries, letters, newspaper items, magazine articles, transcripts of radio interviews, traditional stories, modern short stories, poetry, and extracts from novels and non-fiction books.

Most units consist of at least two passages. These are related in theme but are generally very different in style. For example, in Unit 1 of Book 1 a newspaper item is paired with a traditional story; in Unit 4 a personal letter is paired with an article from an in-flight magazine. This helps students to appreciate differences of writing styles and registers of language. It also provides a wider stimulus for discussion and writing. The last unit in each book consists of a longer and more challenging piece of writing which has been divided into shorter sections for easier study.

In the early stages of learning a foreign language, it is appropriate and indeed necessary that vocabulary and grammatical structures used in reading passages are tightly controlled. A result of this may be language which is rather stilted or unnatural. At the intermediate stage, however, students should be attempting to use 'real' English. In these books, not only the subject matter but also the language level of all passages is such as would be suitable for native English-speaking students of the same age. Rather than simplifying texts, less common words or idiomatic phrases have been retained where their use would be natural in the context, and these words are either glossed at the end of each passage or dealt with in the 'vocabulary work' section.

The units have been arranged with an eye to progression of difficulty and variety of subject matter, but the teacher may choose to vary the order of study of units, perhaps to co-ordinate topics with those being dealt with in other language books, or with other parts of the curriculum.

3: Activities

Pre-reading discussion

This section is intended to engage students' interest in the topic of the unit, and to find out what they already know and think. It sets a purpose for reading.

Vocabulary work

Some vocabulary questions in this section involve multiple choice; others require students to find matching words in the text; and others ask students to provide their own meanings for specified words in the text. Students may also be asked to work out meanings from context, or by identifying 'root' words, prefixes and suffixes. Encourage students to check their 'guesses' with their dictionaries.

Each text offers many opportunities for extending vocabulary. Draw attention, for instance, to words that can be used in more than one sense, eg bank (Unit 4, Book 1). Students can also be made aware of how words can be grouped into 'families'. Words can be members of three types of families. Firstly, they may be part of a family of words made from the same root word: 'prepare', 'preparation' and 'preparatory' are related in this way. Secondly, a word can be grouped with words of similar types of objects: 'leopard' belongs to a family of animal names, 'hammer' to the names of tools. Thirdly, there are families of synonyms, words of the same or similar meaning: 'brave' is part of the 'family' of words like 'courageous', 'bold', 'confident', 'fearless', etc.

Dictionaries are particularly important at the intermediate stage. They are naturally indispensable in vocabulary development. But students need to be trained to use dictionaries with skill and confidence. With this in mind, Unit 2 of Book 1 focuses on the intelligent use of dictionaries, and 'Using your dictionary' exercises are regularly provided in later units. Take care to find the dictionary best suited to the needs of your students. You may wish to consider the *Macmillan Student's Dictionary*, which has been specially compiled for intermediate students and which is used for many of the definitions quoted in this book.

Understanding

Some of the questions in this section require simple *yes / no* or *true / false* answers; others are of multiple choice format; and others test understanding by requiring fuller answers. Whatever the format, students should always be required to justify their answers by close reference to the text, quoting words and phrases which support their answers. When helping students to a better understanding, it is well to keep in mind three common causes of misunderstanding:

a) **connectives.** Expressions like 'because', 'although', 'in case' show how ideas are linked and also determine meaning.

   Compare, for instance:

   'Paul was given the job although / because he was young.'

   'Jane took an umbrella because it was raining / in case it rained.'

b) **qualifying words and phrases.** Compare:

   'All / Some / Few / Many / Most / No TV programmes are boring.'

   'Watching violence on TV (perhaps / maybe) makes people violent in real life.'

   Similar qualifying words and phrases are 'partly', 'hardly', 'scarcely' and 'to some extent'. Again, note the difference between the very common words / phrases 'few' and 'a few'. Compare: 'Joan has few friends' (not many) with 'Joan has a few friends' (several).

c) **negatives, and especially 'double' negatives.** Compare: 'Kim was not unhappy to stay at home' with 'Kim was happy to stay at home' (both positive, but to differing degrees).

Text / paragraph organisation

These sections lay particular emphasis on how different types of writing are organised. Students learn first of all how individual paragraphs are organised, how sentences are related within a paragraph, often with joining words and phrases, and then how paragraphs themselves are connected. They also learn that not all types of writing are organised in the same way. An encyclopaedia entry, a personal letter, or a newspaper story may or may not address similar topics, but they are *organised* in different ways and students need to be made aware of this. A broad distinction can be made between narrative and expository types of writing.

Organisation of narrative

In narrative (fictional stories and accounts of true events), events are usually related in the order in which they happened, although sometimes storytellers, like film-makers, use a 'flashback technique', eg 'Jane read the letter again. She had found it on her office desk two days before.

She had already read it and reread it many times. What did it mean?' But however a story is told, good writers always make clear not only *what* happened, but also *when, where, why, how,* and with *what result* it happened, and *who* was involved. Students need to notice how this is done and be encouraged to achieve similar clarity when writing about events in their own life, whether in personal letters or in making up stories.

Organisation of expository writing

Expository writing, as seen for example in a newspaper article or an encyclopaedia entry, is organised quite differently from narrative. It is with this type of writing that students have most difficulty, both in comprehending text and in being able to write themselves. They need to understand how paragraphs *relate* to each other in order to *develop* an explanation or argument. One useful tool for achieving this is the 'spider' diagram. (See Unit 3 of Book 1, page 29.)

Students need also to understand that in expository writing

a) a well-constructed paragraph has one main topic;

b) this topic is often, *but not always*, stated in a topic sentence;

(If a topic sentence is used, it is frequently placed as the first sentence. The following sentences develop the topic, giving more information about it. This type of paragraph provides an excellent model for students to study. Sometimes, however, the topic sentence is not the first sentence.)

c) sometimes there is no *single* sentence that is clearly the topic sentence.

But the golden rule remains: a paragraph should always be about one main topic.

Pronouns

Some units contain exercises on pronouns. Students need to learn how pronouns relate to nouns. In particular, they must be able to produce written material in which pronoun reference is clear.

Reading aloud

Students should be given opportunities and encouragement to read aloud. Sometimes a story can be made into a dramatised reading. This should only be done when students fully understand what they are reading. Moreover they need explicit instruction in how to read aloud effectively. Certain passages or extracts from passages are suggested in the Student's Book as being particularly suitable for such study and presentation.

Punctuation

A sound understanding of the rules of punctuation enables students both to understand the texts they read and to write clearly themselves. The punctuation exercises may be based on part of a text that has just been read (in which case self-checking is easy), or on a piece of new text related to the topic of the unit. The emphasis is on the most common punctuation marks, in particular full stops and commas. Once these are mastered, getting other marks correct is relatively easy. A short guide to basic punctuation is included in each Student's Book.

Spelling

English spelling is notoriously difficult, even for native speakers. Unfortunately, there are hardly any simple rules which cover large numbers of common words and have few exceptions. Good spelling depends mostly on being able to *visualise* the shape of words. The short spelling sections in each unit are designed to concentrate attention on the most common sources of errors, and some of the most commonly misspelled words. Many exercises are based on words used in the passages, and for these line references provide easy means of self-checking.

Discussion

Students should be encouraged, as appropriate, to give their own opinions and to relate the subject matter of the texts to their own experience and environment. They may well need a good deal of prompting and encouragement, but such discussion, perhaps initially in pairs and groups, then as a class, will provide many fruitful ideas for writing.

Writing

Writing assignments need not be long. They follow naturally from the texts and discussions.

Further reading

Interest in the topics covered in these books should stimulate further reading, and thus an extension of language competence. Encyclopaedias with their short informative articles are particularly useful in this respect. Several excellent ones are now available, in print and in CD-ROM form, specially written for teenage readers.

4: Presentation of the material and organisation of the activities

Many factors are involved in learning and teaching. Experienced and competent teachers in similar conditions often teach equally successfully in very different ways. Much depends on the language competence level of the students, their cultural background, and the preferred teaching styles of the school or college. It is not advisable, however, to have passages read aloud around the class a few lines at a time by students who are quite unprepared and do not really understand *what* they are reading or *how* it should best be read, and then to follow this type of reading by oral questioning around the class. This is because the questions are not matched to students' abilities, and often students are so distracted working out which question theirs will be that they do not pay full attention to what is presently going on in class.

Useful teaching principles

1 Students need to be actively involved in reading, writing and oral work.

2 Tasks can be split between work at school and work at home.

3 Learning should be seen as a co-operative, not a competitive activity, with pair and group work being used in class when appropriate.

4 Students are being taught not tested. They should always be guided towards correct answers.

Pre-reading discussions

Reading of texts and preparation of answers may be done at school or at home, but either way, pre-reading discussions should take place in class before such reading and preparation. (See suggested sequence below.) The amount of time spent on discussion will depend very much on the subject matter of the reading passages. The teacher may prompt responses, but should avoid providing information students will find when they read the text.

Introduction of texts

Texts can be introduced by being read aloud by the teacher. A good reading with appropriate emphases and pauses brings out the meaning and intention of the writer, and is a great help in promoting understanding and arousing interest. This reading aloud should naturally occur *after* the pre-reading discussions, and *before* the individual / group study of the text (whether at school or home), though the teacher may prefer to present the text again after the individual study.

Reading and preparation of texts – individual study

It is recommended that students read and prepare passages carefully *before* they are studied and discussed in class. They should also work out answers to the Vocabulary and Understanding sections, using their dictionaries. Many questions are of the *yes / no* or multiple choice type. Ample line and paragraph references are given, so they are well suited to individual study.

One particular advantage of preparation at home is that students can devote to the task as much time as they require. In class, students who are better at English will finish their preparation well ahead of weaker students. On the other hand, there are various advantages to preparation of material in class, among them being that there are times when the teacher wants to see students individually, perhaps to discuss corrected work while the rest of the students are preparing texts. The teacher might also want to circulate round the class to help weaker students in their preparation.

Classwork activities

The questions in the Vocabulary and Understanding sections are of varying levels of difficulty. Try to match particular questions with the abilities of individual students, rather than just working up and down the rows of desks. Many of the questions provided can be taken as starting points for further questions, based on students' own interests, experience and linguistic abilities. Some suggestions for such supplementary questions are included in these teacher's notes.

Work on paragraph and text structure, spelling and punctuation, as well as discussion of the topics, all help to further the study of the reading passages, and also prepare students for their own writing assignments. The amount of writing required will depend very much on individual ability. However, it is better to have shorter and more frequent writing assignments than longer and less frequent ones.

When writing assignments have been marked, it is always useful to have a follow-up session when for at least part of a lesson students can read out their pieces, and the teacher can discuss common errors.

A suggested teaching sequence

The following sequence, based on the previous notes, is merely a framework which the teacher can vary according to circumstances and to the type of reading passage being studied. Work on the texts has been divided into five stages. Three should be done as a whole class. The other two involve individual work at home, or individual / pair / group work at school.

1 At school (whole class)

Pre-reading discussion, followed perhaps by reading of the text by the teacher.

2 At school (individual / pair work / small group study) or as homework

Students read texts and prepare answers. Encourage use of dictionaries. Students should identify difficulties with which they may need the teacher's help. If this work is done in class, the teacher may circulate, helping weaker students in particular.

3 At school (whole class)

a) The text is (again) presented by the teacher. Students are then invited to answer questions and work on vocabulary development. The teacher can also ask supplementary questions based on the Understanding section. Students can ask about problems they have experienced with the work.
b) Discussion of the structure of individual paragraphs and of the text as a whole.
c) Reading aloud as indicated in the Student's Book, or decided by the teacher.
d) Discussion based on the topics suggested.
e) Punctuation and spelling exercises are completed.
f) Preparatory work, as necessary, for writing. The teacher can help with ideas and vocabulary and can suggest how pieces may be structured.

4 At home or school (individual work)

Students complete their short writing assignment.

5 At school (whole class)

a) Individuals may read out their writing assignments (now corrected), or the teacher may prefer to read out selected extracts.
b) The teacher can use this opportunity to deal with persistent errors of word use, grammar, punctuation or spelling that the writing assignments have shown to be most common.

English Reading and Comprehension

Teacher's Book 1

Contents

Water, water everywhere!

An incredible rescue

Explain to students that this report is taken without any change from an English newspaper. This should increase their confidence from the outset regarding their developing competence in reading *authentic* English texts.

Pre-reading discussion

3 Suggest students try to find seven precautions. You might ask them to work co-operatively in groups.

Suggestions: (1) If you are not a good swimmer, do not swim out of your depth (so that you can stand up if necessary). (2) Even if you are a good swimmer do not swim too far from the shore. (3) Avoid strong currents in rivers and the sea. (4) Never swim alone. (5) It is best to have someone on shore to watch you and call for help or come to your rescue if there are problems. (6) Do not swim soon after a meal. (7) Parents should be in the water with young children at all times.

Vocabulary work

Headline

1 sightless

Point out that 'blind' is the usual word to use for a person who cannot see. 'Sightless' is not the regular word; students should not use it. Note however that 'sighted' (line 47) is the regular word for a person who is not blind. The headline writer has used 'sightless' so that it alliterates with the initial 's' sounds in '*s*wimmer *s*aves *s*urfer'. Alliteration (repetition of the same consonant sound) is common in poetry (see Unit 5, page 44). As well as in headlines, alliteration is also used in advertising because it sounds attractive and makes the words memorable.

Paragraph 1

2 roar (line 2)

3 a) drag (line 17)
  b) rescue (line 4)
  c) totally (line 6)
  d) really (line 6)
  e) help (line 2)

4 c) a very brave person

5 'Hero' describes a brave man; 'heroine' describes a brave woman.

6 tide (line 16)

7 A battle is a fight between armies or large groups of soldiers. He had great difficulty in swimming; he had to 'fight' the sea, which was like an enemy in war.

8 c) at once

9 a) smooth / calm
  b) safe

Paragraph 2

10 eventually (line 30)

11 to take hold very firmly

12 two

13 shore (line 31)

Paragraph 3

14 beach (line 38)

Paragraphs 4 and 5

15 a) an object rather like a coin and often on a ribbon
  b) metal – often gold or silver
  c) Medals are usually given to people as a reward, often for bravery.

You may ask students what awards and medals are given in their own country.

Understanding

1 a) True – it tells how a brave blind person saved a swimmer from drowning. (lines 3–6)
b) False – we are told he is 43 years old and has been blind for 22 years. (lines 7 and 11)
c) True (line 12)
d) True (lines 1–6)
e) False – it was the rescuer who was blind. (lines 5–6 and 10–11)
f) False – it was Patrick Slack who had been surfing (line 12); David Hurst had been swimming. (line 20)
g) True (line 16)
h) False – his son was with him, not swimming in the water, but playing on the beach. (line 37)
i) False – the coastguards arrived 'after the rescue'. (line 43)
j) False – Coastguard Allan Lloyd said David Hurst *deserved* a medal; he had been so brave he should get one (line 45). But we do not know whether in fact he did get one.

2 c) swimming (line 20)

3 b) He did not hesitate about going into the sea.

4 The wind was so strong (line 16) and the sea was roaring. (line 2)

5 a) David Hurst asked Patrick Slack where he was, so indicating that he could not see. (lines 38–39)
b) Sea water is salty.

6 the rough sea (line 29), the tide and the strong wind (line 33)

7 The rescuers might get drowned themselves.

Pronouns

1 David Hurst
2 Patrick Slack
3 the coastguards
4 David Hurst
5 Patrick Slack
6 Patrick Slack and David Hurst

The boatman and the professor

Pre-reading discussion

2 **Elicit that there may be great practical difficulties in teaching certain skills at school, however useful, for example finding qualified teachers, having suitable facilities available and making time for learning them (time for other subjects would be cut). Consider the four skills separately. First aid might be most easily fitted in, but swimming and life-saving would require access to a swimming pool and fully qualified instructors. Learning to drive a car would be the most impracticable.**

Vocabulary work

Paragraph 1

1 a) slowly (line 2)
b) small (line 2)
c) clever (line 1)
d) wide (line 3)

2 a) at last (line 4)
b) silent (line 3)

Paragraph 3

3 boring / uninteresting. (Elicit 'boring' as a common and useful word.)

4 c) well known. Examples: The pyramids of Egypt are famous. / Abraham Lincoln was a famous American president.

5 a) combat between large armies

You may like to refer back to 'battle' used as a verb in the earlier part of this unit (line 13, page 5, and question 7 in Vocabulary work, page 6).

b) Answers depend on students' knowledge.

6 a) old (grandfather)

b) ancient (Greeks)

c) ancient (civilisations)

d) old (house)

Note the meaning of 'ancient' is explained in the Vocabulary on page 8.

Paragraph 4

7 Unfortunately

Explain if necessary that 'I am afraid ...' is very common in English in expressions such as:

I am afraid I cannot come to your party. / I am afraid I have some bad news for you.

Paragraph 7

8 a) far off (line 18)

b) precious (line 19)

Paragraph 10

9 a) They were getting closer together.

10 There is a lot of wind and rain (or snow).

11 a) the side of a river

b) a sloping piece of ground, not necessarily by a river; a place where people keep their money

Paragraphs 12,13 and 14

12 a) saved (line 38)

b) maybe (line 34)

c) trembling (line 30)

d) enough (line 34)

e) started (line 36)

f) chose (line 35)

13 a child whose parents are dead

14 The word 'grab' suggests holding or taking something suddenly and violently.

You may like to refer back to the news item on page 5, line 31 and question 11, page 6.

15 a) poor (line 32)

b) large (line 33)

16 did not have enough money

Understanding

1 a) False – it sank because of the storm (line 36). It is not likely that the boatman would be using a boat too small for only two people!

b) False – the boatman could not read at all. (line 12)

c) False – he did not learn because he did not go to school. He says that maybe he will learn soon. (paragraph 13)

d) False – she was too poor to send him to school. (line 33)

e) True – the professor says the boatman's life is 'hardly worth living' and that he 'might as well be dead'. (paragraph 9)

f) True – 'the professor could not remain silent for long' (lines 3–4)

g) False – the professor had never learned to swim. (line 30)

h) and i) False – we are not told why the boatman saved the professor's life. We assume it was simply because the boatman was a good man.

j) False – we are not told whether the professor rewarded the boatman.

2 The boatman would have needed oars for rowing. (An oar is a long pole with a shaped board at the end which is used to move a boat through the water – see the picture, page 8.)

3 a) The river was wide, so the boatman had a long way to row and would not have hurried. Moreover he had a passenger in the boat, which would have reduced his speed.

b) There was not enough time for the boat to reach the bank before the storm started. The storm was the reason why the boat sank.

4 a) The boatman had not read any history.
  b) 2 unfortunate

Point out that if we feel pity for people, we feel sorry for them, for example if they are poor or ill.

5 Perhaps because he was a teacher and liked to explain things to people.

6 a) Europe / Africa / Asia / America / Australia
  b) Mount Everest. (Ask why this mountain is special – it is the highest mountain in the world.)
  c) the Amazon (S America) / the Nile (Egypt) / the Mississippi (USA) / the Ganges (India) / the Thames (UK – London is on the Thames) / the Seine (France – Paris is on the Seine)
  d) iron, gold, silver, copper
  e) pepper, paprika, cinnamon
  f) diamonds, emeralds, rubies

7 the boat has sunk (paragraph 14); there is a storm (paragraph 14); they are only halfway across a wide river (paragraph 10)

8 Part 1: paragraphs 1–9, Part 2: paragraphs 10–14. In Part 1 the weather is good and the professor feels happy and superior to the boatman. In Part 2 the storm comes and the professor becomes very frightened and has to rely on the boatman to save his life.

Discussion

1,2 **Ask students how they would describe the men. We are told the professor is clever (line 1) and very talkative (lines 3–4). He is proud and impolite, but elicit he is not a bad man. He feels sorry for the boatman. The boatman wants to learn and is a brave man, who risks his own life to save the professor.**

3 **The story does not suggest learning history and geography is a waste of time. Both subjects sound interesting as described by the professor. Certainly we should all learn something about history, particularly the history of our own country and culture and also about other countries in the world. Also, the boatman wishes to learn to read – he regrets he was not able to go to school. But the story also suggests that other skills are worthy of respect and many are necessary like swimming; being able to row a boat is a useful skill. You may wish to invite students to suggest other examples of useful and necessary skills, such as driving a bus or taxi, or cooking. We should not think such activities are inferior, or the people who do them for a living are lesser human beings.**

Spelling

teacher	inspector	driver
solicitor	lawyer	carpenter
doctor	tailor	butcher
author	employer	tractor
helicopter	editor	sailor
photographer	farmer	emperor
spectator	governor	

Have students use their dictionaries to check their spellings and also to learn the meaning of any words which are new to them.

UNIT 2

The tool every reader needs

A short history

Pre-reading discussion

1 spelling, meaning, pronunciation of words

Accept other types of information if offered, but do not suggest further information, which the students will read about in the unit.

2 Count how many headwords there are on five different pages. Divide by five to get the average number. Multiply by the number of pages in the dictionary.

Vocabulary work

Paragraph 1

1 a) unusual (line 8)
b) common (line 7)

Paragraph 2

2 a) started (line 13)
b) aim (line 14)
c) provided (line 18)
d) illustrate (line 18)
e) complete (line 27)
f) increased (line 29)
g) latest (line 30)

3 expert (line 12)

4 a) 1 change
b) verb

5 b) a few words or sentences

Paragraph 3

6 different (line 37)

7 enlarged (line 49)

Paragraph 4

8 a) vital (line 50)
b) excellent (line 51)
c) regularly (line 57)

9 differ (be different)

10 a) hammer, screwdriver, spanner, drill, chisel, plane, spade, shovel, hoe, etc.
b) A tool helps us to carry out a task, and in the same way a dictionary helps us to understand what we read.

Understanding

1 a) False – 'they contained *only* rare words' (line 3)
b) False – the first dictionaries were 'written *before* the 18th century'. (line 2)
c) False – 1755 is in the eighteenth century. (line 5)
d) False – it contained *both* common *and* uncommon words. (lines 7–8)
e) True – 1858 is in the nineteenth century. (line 12)
f) True – it 'took hundreds of people'. (line 26)
g) True – 'number of English words ... increased' (lines 28–29)
h) True (lines 16–17)
i) False – they spoke English, but with some differences. (lines 34–37)
j) True – 'these spellings are still used in America today' (lines 46–47)
k False – 'every reader' needs a dictionary. (line 51)
l) False – we need to get the 'best dictionary for our needs' (lines 55–56) – which might not be the most expensive one we can afford.

Can students suggest when the most expensive might not be the most suitable? Suggest, if necessary, they look at lines 30–33. A very big dictionary might be unnecessarily detailed, particularly for a young person or an overseas learner just starting to learn English. It might also be too heavy to carry around. A smaller one, maybe with pictures and special help for foreign learners, might be much better, though cheaper.

2 The makers of the dictionaries believed readers would not need to look up very common words such as 'table', 'house', 'cat' as they would know what these things were, and they could also spell them.

Ask: Isn't this a good idea – why shouldn't dictionaries still be like that? Elicit that the problem is knowing for sure what a common word is. Adults will know words that children will not yet have heard or read. Also, we all have different special interests and special knowledge, eg gained through our jobs and hobbies, and so we will have a wider vocabulary in these areas. Therefore what is a common word for some people will not be a common word for other people; and for people learning English as a foreign language all words are at first uncommon! Similarly, it is rarely possible to say which words are simple to spell: even short common words may be difficult (eg 'knife'), and some people are better spellers than others.

3 the, house, man. They are all very common words, and not very difficult to spell.

4 a) It included common words as well as rare ones.

b) It showed how words should be used in sentences.

5 a) It included all words, even those that were no longer used and it gave information about when words were first used and which languages they came from.

Explain that English is mainly a mixture of languages that were spoken in Northern Europe many centuries ago, but that over time words have been added from nearly every country in the world because in the past English merchants sailed all round the world and England had a large empire.

b) It took so long to write because the dictionary included all the words in English, including many no longer used, together with many quotations from writers showing how the words were used. It therefore took many people many years to collect and organise all these words and meanings, especially as many words in English can have more than one meaning.

6 We might come across words which are no longer used if we were reading books written in the past.

7 a) It gave the meanings of words used in America.

b) It gave simplified spellings of words, which are now used as standard by American writers.

8 Words are being added to the language all the time, for example names of new inventions.

Ask whether students might be able to give some examples, eg photograph, photography, telephone, radio, aeroplane, television, typewriter, computer.

9 a) plow, center, color

Paragraphing

1 a) English dictionaries before the nineteenth century. This title *includes* both topics (b) and (c).

2 a) *The Oxford English Dictionary*

b) *Webster's Dictionary of American English*

3 c) Dictionaries are essential for all readers.

Pronouns

a) Dr Samuel Johnson's famous dictionary (lines 6–7)

b) language experts (line 12)

c) language experts (line 12)

d) The OED (*The Oxford English Dictionary*) (line 22)

e) Americans (line 34)

f) Noah Webster (lines 41–42)

g) dictionaries (line 52)

Spelling

library	mystery	primary
factory	machinery	vocabulary
robbery	satisfactory	secretary
memory	mercury	

Bringing language to life

Parts of speech

1 n. – noun, v. – verb, adj. – adjective, adv. – adverb, prep. – preposition, conj. – conjunction

2 noun

3 three – adjective, noun, verb

Note the adverb, 'finely'. Remind students how adverbs can often be made from English adjectives by adding '-ly'. Ask for examples: quickly, badly, nearly, poorly, etc.

4 one

Example sentences

1 a) noun and adjective. (Explain 'stable' may be used less commonly as a verb, as in: The horses were stabled in a shed behind the house.)

b) adjective

2 a) The weather is fine at the moment.

b) If you park your car on this line, you may have to pay a fine.

Different grammatical forms of verbs

1 irregular verb

2 a) shook

b) shaking

c) shaken

3 see – seeing, saw, seen (irregular)
buy – buying, bought, bought (irregular)
say – saying, said, said (irregular)
talk – talking, talked, talked (regular)
ride – riding, rode, ridden (irregular)
fight – fighting, fought, fought (irregular)
hope – hoping, hoped, hoped (regular)
hop – hopping, hopped, hopped (regular)
freeze – freezing, froze, frozen (irregular)
become – becoming, became, become (irregular)
drink – drinking, drank, drunk (irregular)

It is clear that this sort of information helps with the spelling of irregular verbs, but point out / elicit how it can help with the spelling of regular verbs, for example the doubling of a final consonant (see 'hop' above) or dropping of final 'e' as in 'hope'.

Syllables and stress

1 three syllables

2 a) metaphor

b) simile

c) metaphor

3 a) the first syllable

b) by using *italic*

c) simplified spelling

4 boy (one syllable), woman (two), beautiful (three), Egypt (two), cat (one), reply (two), dictation (three), cigarette (three), departure (three), unkindly (three)

5 **An open question, but italic and underlining make it immediately clear which the stressed syllable is. (With a stress mark you have to remember whether the dictionary places this before or after the stressed syllable.) Some students may feel italic 'stands out' more than underlining, especially if the print is small.**

6 a) italic
b) noun and verb
c) two syllables – it uses a space

Ask if students know what 'dessert' means – sweet food eaten at the end of a meal. (This noun has the same pronunciation as 'desert' (v), but is written with a double 's'.) You may ask what the students' favourite desserts are. Can they describe them in English?

Showing which other language a word has come from

Dutch

Help with grammar and spelling

1 equipment, information, sugar

Elicit / explain that for the plurals of these words one has to use phrases, eg *pieces of* equipment; *items of* information; *teaspoons / packets of* sugar.

2 phonetic alphabet
3 verb and noun
4 a soft vegetable; a game played, usually by two players, with rackets and a ball, on a walled indoor court. (Note 'squash' can also be used as a noun in the following sense: There were six passengers in the tiny car. It was such a squash.)

Saying how formal or informal a word is

phonetic script

Illustrations

1 especially
2 phonetic alphabet
3 Yes, it would be impossible to imagine what a chariot looks like from a simple description in words.

Some dictionary entries

1 **fridge** – a) part of speech (noun)
d) pronunciation i) illustration
(Students might feel the illustration is not very useful – they know very well what a fridge looks like.)

2 **squawk** – a) part of speech (verb)
b) example sentence

3 **fan** – a) parts of speech (noun and verb)
g) help with grammar / spelling – making the plural form of the noun, and parts of the verb (doubling of 'n') i) illustration

Ask if 'fan' is a regular or irregular verb – regular. It might be interesting to take a vote on how useful students find the illustration to be.

4 **check** – a) parts of speech (verb and adjective) b) example sentences

Note 'cheque': a piece of paper telling a bank to pay someone a sum of money. (In American English the spelling 'check' is used.)

5 **equip** – a) part of speech (verb)
b) example sentences c) different forms of verbs d) pronunciation (Method is simplified spelling.) e) stress (Indicated with a stress mark before the stressed syllable.) g) help with grammar / spelling ('With' after 'equipped' is printed in heavy type to remind students of the correct preposition needed.)

Ask if this a regular or irregular verb – regular verb. Ask what help is given with spelling – past tense and past participle have double 'p'. Note the entry also gives 'equipment' (many dictionaries would make this a separate entry). Ask what grammatical help is given with this word – that equipment cannot be used in the plural.

6 **equator** – d) pronunciation
e) syllables and stress i) illustration

Ask how syllables and stress are indicated – there are three syllables, and a space indicates that the main break / pause occurs after the first one. Usefulness of the illustration may be disputed.

7 an open question

All that glitters

Choose carefully!

Check if students know 'glitter' – to shine. Explain that the title is the first three words of a famous English proverb. Ask if they know the next three. Most probably they will not, so leave the question until they have read the story and have finished the questions and discussion. If they still do not know the answer, give them next two words – 'is not' – and ask for the final word – 'gold'. Explain that the proverb means that just because something looks valuable (shiny, like gold) on the outside, it does not mean it is truly worth having.

Vocabulary work

Section 1

1 poor (line 2)

2 a poor person who asks for food or money, especially in the street

Section 2

3 perfectly (line 21), quite (line 24)

4 generous (line 19)

Section 3a

5 glistening (line 32)

6 forgot

Section 3b

7 shock (line 35)

Section 3c

8 alarm (line 42)

Ask students if they know 'fire alarm', 'burglar alarm'.

9 a) a very quick movement

b) holding very tightly

c) shouting with a high, sharp-sounding voice

Section 3d

10 wise (line 50)

11 b) wealth (line 52); riches (line 53)

12 a representation of a person made of stone or metal

13 at once (lines 31 and 42), immediately (line 37), in an instant (line 48)

Understanding

1 a) False – it was the poor man that was hungry. (line 3)

b) False – he was 'kind-hearted'. (lines 4–5)

c) False – he was only given a few silver coins for food (lines 5–6). He did not buy the clothes with this money – he changed into a richly dressed man by magic.

d) False – 'you did not make a wise choice' (lines 49–50)

e) False – 'he shouted out in fear' (line 38)

f) False – she was frightened 'when she heard her father shout out' (lines 40–42). She did not have time to run away: '*at once* she too turned to solid gold' (lines 42–43).

g) False – the magician said: 'You are a good man'. (line 49)

h) False – the story take places on three days. The first day the prince meets the beggar (line 2). The next day he meets him again, now dressed in rich silk clothes (lines 9–10). The wish to turn anything he touches into gold is granted the prince the following day (line 28).

i) False – the father did not realise that his daughter would be turned into gold – he 'shrieked' and was distressed. (lines 44–47)

j) False – the prince had to bathe to lose his power of turning things into gold as a cure, not as a punishment. (line 58)

2 They tell the story of the prince bathing in the river to lose his power of turning anything he touched into gold.

3 a) The man was dressed in silk clothes and was riding a horse.

b) He said that he was the man the prince had given money to the previous day. How could this be? The prince was perhaps also surprised at being offered repayment. (line 11)

4 Whether he would be kind to a poor beggar. Yes, he passed this test.

5 A test to see if he could choose wisely. No, he failed.

6 He asked that *everything* would change to gold. He forgot about the need to touch food and people.

7 'Choose carefully' (line 17) suggests a warning; 'without thinking' (line 20) suggests the prince is making a bad choice; the magician asks if the prince is 'quite sure' (line 22), all of which suggest to us that a mistake is going to be made.

8 Because the prince was really a good man, as shown when he gave money to the magician disguised as a beggar.

Spelling

either	brief	field
weight	ceiling	niece
receipt	thief	conceit
chief	fierce	deceive
receive	belief	pierce

Students should use their dictionaries to check their spellings and to make sure they understand what the words mean.

How stories are told

1 a) Why a certain river contains gold – section 4

b) A foolish choice – section 2

c) A generous prince – section 1

d) Joy and despair! – section 3

2 a) All ends well! – 3d

b) The prince is delighted – 3a

c) Disaster! – 3c

d) Gold for breakfast – 3b

Newspaper stories

A newspaper story is organised so that the reader can understand immediately what it is about and decide if he will read further and learn more details. Ask students what the headline and first sentence of the story of the prince and the magician might be if it was reported by a newspaper. One suggestion is:

Prince's daughter turned to gold

Yesterday a prince's daughter turned into a solid gold statue – simply at her father's touch – and stayed like that for three hours.

Discussion

1 **Note there may be disagreement here at what is surprising and what is not.**

(1) Some students may suggest that the kindness of the prince is surprising, as we might expect princes to be proud. But in fact there is no reason why they should be. Everyone should agree it is surprising (2) that the man in silk clothes and on a horse should be the same as the beggar, (3) that he was a magician, (4) that he could offer such a great reward: *anything* the prince wanted. Some students may say that (5) the prince's choice of wish is surprising, but perhaps we might think this *only after knowing what happens*. Certainly surprising is (6) that articles can in fact change to gold – though in this sort of story everything is possible, and we might expect this. Students will probably be surprised (7) that food and

water, and then the prince's daughter, change to gold. Elicit how they probably had not thought of the consequences. Students may be further surprised (8) that the magician appears instantly, and (9) maybe that he helps the prince – but then the prince had been kind to the 'beggar'.

2 The magician says what the 'lesson' is in lines 51–54. But the title 'Choose carefully', echoed also in line 17, also suggests a lesson – that we should always think hard of the consequences of our actions (what might happen) before we do something.

Punctuation

Remind students that though it is *always* clear when a full stop (or a question or exclamation mark) is necessary, the placing of commas is sometimes a matter of choice. Therefore all the full stops are needed as in the text. Many writers would put a comma after 'ago' in the first line, but it is not necessary. A comma after 'coins' in the last sentence is not optional. A comma after 'prince' (line 7) is optional but would be rarely used today. See also the Basic punctuation guide in the Student's Book on page 92, section 5(b).

The most precious metal

Vocabulary work

Paragraph 1

1 beautiful (line 8)

2 a) drawn out (line 6)
 b) glowing (line 2)
 c) easy (line 2)
 d) therefore (line 7)
 e) fine (line 6)

3 a) hard
 b) thick

4 Wire is made from metal; string is made from fibre (like rope).

Ask what the difference is between string and rope and which is much thicker and stronger – rope.

Paragraph 2

5 a) precious (line 15)
 b) prized (line 11)
 c) luckily (line 14)
 d) believed (line 12)
 e) skilful (line 18)
 f) objects (line 15)

6 a) 1 a place where someone is buried.

Explain that 'grave' is currently more common – but we usually use 'tomb' to describe where people were buried in ancient times.

 2 a place where interesting and valuable objects from the past are kept and shown.
 3 a person who makes things from gold
 b) A silversmith makes things from silver.

Paragraph 3

7 usually (line 27)

8 a) dearer / more expensive
 b) softer

Paragraph 4

9 rare (line 1)

10 c) common

Paragraph 5

11 also (line 47); too (line 48)

12 obtain

Paragraph 6

13 c) unpleasant brightness

Understanding

1 a) False – *also* to make it harder, not just cheaper (line 29)

b) False – it is the softness of gold which makes it suitable for gold leaf (lines 4–5). Mixing makes it harder (line 29).

c) False – it is 'still used today'. (line 23)

d) False – one third pure gold would be 8 carat (24/3). (lines 31–34)

e) False – we are not told the reasons, but the idea is ridiculous.

f) False – the article says gold could be extracted, but it would be too costly. (line 49)

g) False – two thirds of the gold is in banks. (lines 42–44)

h) False – it is used as a shield from the glare of the sun. (line 57)

i) True (lines 36–37)

j) False – the Pharaohs were kings. (line 13)

k) False – practical uses only mentioned for modern times (last paragraph).

l) False – the reason for not using gold nowadays is not given.

Remind students that they must answer according to information given in the passage.

2 a) *around* the neck

b) *on* a finger

Point out the correct prepositions.

3 'rare' (line 1)

4 It is not affected by air or water. (lines 3–4)

5 Yes, because pure gold is soft and easy to beat into sheets.

6 22 carat is more valuable because it contains more gold. An 18-carat gold ring would be three quarters (75%) gold (18/24).

7 Paper money is more convenient. It is much lighter. A very large amount of money can be represented by the same size of paper as a very small amount of money. Silver was also used – mentioned on page 22, line 6. Coins made of valuable metal would be readily accepted in other countries – important in ancient times when there were no banks. You can forge paper money more successfully than metal coins – it is easier to detect if a coin is not made of pure gold or silver.

8 A person who is qualified to look after teeth. He practises dentistry. Gold is very suitable as it is not affected by air and water (lines 3–4) – the mouth is always moist – and gold can also be easily moulded (line 5).

Pronouns

1 gold

2 the ancient Egyptians

3 people living today

4 gold

5 countries

Paragraphs

paragraph 2: Gold in ancient Egypt

paragraph 3: Mixing gold with other metals

paragraph 4: Using gold for money

paragraph 5: Where gold is found

paragraph 6: Modern practical uses for gold

Using spiders

a) Gold is used for pen nibs – with <u>Modern practical uses</u> – paragraph 6

b) The museums in Cairo are world famous – with <u>In Egypt</u> – paragraph 2

c) Roman gold coins are very interesting and valuable – with <u>As money</u> – paragraph 4

d) Many stories have been written in which gold plays an important part – as there is nothing about topic (d) in the spider, it would make an additional paragraph in the finished article, suggested topic title: <u>Stories about gold</u>. The article would then consist of seven paragraphs.

Ask where this additional paragraph might go. Elicit that it would not be the first paragraph. The existing one is a good introductory paragraph. As the other paragraphs are all about decorative and practical uses of gold, the paragraph on stories might be added at the end. Or it might go between paragraphs 5 and 6.

UNIT 4

Going places

Please write soon!

Pre-reading discussion

There are Disney theme parks in the United States, France and Japan. (They have different names, but always including 'Disney'.) They offer a variety of exciting events and rides based on Disney films. By the time he died in 1966 Walt Disney had become the most famous name in children's entertainment, especially in cartoon films. Ask for names and other details of his films (eg *Snow White and the Seven Dwarfs*, *Bambi*, *Pinocchio*, *101 Dalmatians*, *The Jungle Book*).

Vocabulary work

Paragraph 1

1 e) very bad

Paragraph 2

2 e) quite

Paragraph 3

3 a) fortunately (line 13)

b) a line of people waiting for something

Paragraph 4

4 a) younger

Explain that 'elder' / 'eldest' mean 'older' / 'oldest' but are used only of family relationships, especially brother and sister. Ask how many brothers must Louise have – two, as the comparative ending '-er' is used when only two things are compared. If she had more than two brothers, she would have written 'eldest' ('eld' does not exist in modern English).

b) excellent

Explain that 'great' is commonly used in this sense, particularly in speech and informal writing.

c) wonderful (line 6), marvellous (line 15), superb (line 26)

d) large in size, number or importance. Examples: Paris is a great city. / Shakespeare is a great English writer.

Paragraph 5

5 a) also (line 21)

b) Example: Would you dare to make a parachute jump?

Paragraph 6

6 parades (line 24)

Paragraph 7

7 loved (line 27), adores (line 27)

Some students may suggest 'like' (line 29) as one of the pair of words, but explain that 'loved' and 'adores' are both stronger words, and so make the best pair.

Paragraph 8

8 a) perhaps

b) Examples: I am looking forward to my birthday. / My sister is looking forward to her wedding.

Understanding

1 a) False – *Louise* has had the birthday. She received the present for which she is now thanking Fatima. (line 6)

b) True (line 7)

c) False – 'none of us' (line 8)

d) False – Louise refers to her 'last letter'. (line 10)

e) True – 'it was so crowded' (line 13)

f) True – Ask what her name is – Annette. (lines 15–16)

2 'I know so little about you as yet' (lines 31–32) and 'I'm sure we're going to be great penfriends'. (lines 32–33)

3 a) The Florida theme park is bigger (line 11) and the weather is sunnier (line 14).

b) France is nearer to England – it is easier and cheaper to travel to.

4 Both are held at night – when it is dark.

5 She probably read about it in a guide book. (line 25)

Organising a personal letter

Louise's main topic is her visit to Disneyland with her family.

Paragraph 1

a) Louise thought the present was wonderful. The letter included an account of Fatima's sister's wedding. Louise received pictures of the wedding with the letter.

b) Louise believes that she is very bad at French. Louise thinks Fatima writes good English.

Paragraph 2

the size of Disneyland

Paragraph 3

a) It can be crowded – there were long queues when Louise went.

b) The weather may not be good. (This is suggested by the word 'fortunately' and by the comparison with Florida.)

Paragraph 4

a) 'There are great things to see.' (line 15)

b) We are then told what the great things are.

Ask how many 'great things' Louise chooses to mention and what they are – Sleeping Beauty's Castle, Frontierland, pirates of the Caribbean area.

Paragraph 5

a) The rides that are available.

b) Yes – 'There are some great rides too.' (line 20)

c) too

Elicit that paragraph 4 is about things to see, places to visit; and paragraph 5 is about rides you can take.

Paragraph 6

a) Disney characters walking around, parades, fireworks

b) 'How do you know how many light bulbs there are?' or 'Did you count the light bulbs?' or 'How were you able to / could you count the light bulbs?'

Paragraph 7

The flowers and trees in Disneyland

Paragraph 8

All the questions are linked because they are about different aspects of Fatima's life.

Punctuation

3 a) Do you like swimming?

b) I adore cartoon films!

c) I hate maths!

d) Do you hate maths?

e) When do you return to school?

f) I wish I could go to Disneyland!

Spelling

1 photos

Although there is no rule, older English words generally take the '-oes' ending, and newer words the '-os' ending. The examples illustrate this.

2 a) wonderful (line 1)

b) already (line 31)

You may like to point out the difference between these two sentences:

By ten o'clock, we were all ready for bed.

We were already in bed when the clock struck ten.

A journey back in time

Pre-reading discussion

The questions are mainly open-ended, but you might want to prompt students about their own history and sites of historical importance: What do you know about ...? If students cannot guess what a living museum might be, do not tell them – just say that you are going to read about such a museum now. Then immediately after reading the passage you can ask: Now can you say why the Pharaonic Village is called a living museum?

From an in-flight airline magazine (end of page 38): Elicit / explain that airlines publish magazines for their passengers which tell them about places the airlines serve.

Vocabulary

Pharaonic / Pharaoh – does the students' dictionary give the pronunciation?

fer - *on* - ic / *fair* - o

Vocabulary work

Paragraph 2

1 a) no doubt (line 4)
  b) a trip (line 6)
  c) bargains (line 8)

2 modern (line 8)

Paragraph 4

3 a) drawn (line 17)
  b) trampling (line 19)
  c) tossed (line 21)
  d) bustles (line 28)

4 round, circular

5 a) pottery. (Ask for examples: bowls, jugs, plates, cups, saucers, etc.)
  b) cloth

6 a baker

7 a) ox
  b) child – children, man – men, woman – women

Paragraph 5

8 famous (line 34)

9 artificial (line 39)

Paragraph 6

10 a) ambition (line 46)
  b) gather (line 52)
  c) researching (line 56)

Paragraph 7

11 work / labour

Pronouns

a) Dr Ragab (line 34)
b) Disneyland (line 36)
c) a real Egyptian village (lines 40–41)
d) grain (line 22)

Understanding

1 a) A great river in Egypt
  b) in / on a boat.

Explain that we generally use 'in' for small boats, 'on' for large boats.

2 Cairo (line 47)

3 a) the Sphinx, the pyramids of Giza, the Nile, modern shops, traditional markets
  b) They are very well known.
  c) No, not so famous.

4 a) Wooden ploughs were used in ancient times, before metal was discovered.
  b) steel
  c) by tractors

5 No, he felt Disneyland was unnatural.

6 No, because Cairo would remind visitors of the modern world.

7 They gave him details of life in ancient Egypt.

8 Because Dr Ragab had to find out so much about the past and collect or make many things.

You may like to ask students to give details, which are in paragraph 6.

9 a) the United States
   b) a state

10 probably Egyptian – 'your stay with us' (line 1)

11 the airline

Paragraph / Writing styles

1 a) paragraph 5
   b) paragraph 4
   c) paragraph 6

2 paragraph 4 is mainly descriptive; paragraphs 5 and 6 are mainly explanatory

3 a) paragraphs 3 and 7
   b) to visit the Pharaonic Village

Ask what the purpose of the first two paragraphs is. Elicit that they are introductory. The writer is establishing a friendly relationship with the reader, as in a conversation or personal letter. He is establishing the general topic of places the visitors to Egypt might want to see, first by mentioning well-known places. The 'living museum' of the Pharaonic Village is then introduced as somewhere both interesting and different.

Punctuation

You could ask (1) why capital letters are used for Pharaonic Village – because this is the name of a particular place and (2) why exclamation marks are used in paragraphs 1 and 2 – because the writer is using a very direct and personal style to suggest lively speech; these sentences might be spoken as exclamations.

Spelling

autumn	answer	dumb
climb	design	wrist
fasten	handsome	foreign
scene	chemist	wreck
sign	thumb	knock
often	half	lamb
pneumatic	psychology	

Writing

2 This topic provides a good opportunity for students to work in pairs, first orally, then making notes.

UNIT 5

Put it into words

Take off with books

Pre-reading discussion

Students should have plenty of comments to contribute here – even if they are not great readers; they must have seen a lot of films and TV. The relative advantages of TV, cinema and books are dealt with in the passage on page 47. Accept students' comments but do not guide them here in anticipation of their reading of that passage.

If students are not used to reading poems in English, you should explain that most poems are written rather differently from prose (eg articles, stories, letters and newspaper items). In particular:

- unusual words may be used for effect, including words no longer used in modern English. Four are noted in this poem in the Vocabulary;
- words may be arranged in an unusual order, though in this poem the order of words should not cause problems;
- writers often use rhyme and alliteration to make poems sound more interesting and attractive. There are short exercises on these techniques on page 44. You may want to remind students of the use of alliteration in newspaper headlines (see Unit 1, Vocabulary work, question 1, page 10);
- poets sometimes use less punctuation.

Vocabulary work

a) take off (line 1) b) soar (line 4)

c) beneath (line 7)

Understanding

1 a) roar (line 2)

b) a reader reads silently to himself / herself.

2 Ogden Nash compares reading to travelling in a rocket.

3 **Students could find this a difficult question. Here is a definition they can be helped towards.**

A rocket is a device which is propelled by the burning of some kind of explosive material. Small rockets are used as fireworks. Larger ones can be used, eg on a ship, to signal an emergency (distress rockets). Rockets can carry rope up a cliff or across a gorge when building a bridge. Large ones are used as weapons or to carry spacecraft into space.

4 a very high speed

5 Because these are worlds that we imagine. They can be set in the past and the future. No rocket can travel to places only imagined, or travel in time.

6 We can read about going to the moon in a book. Many authors made up stories about the moon before man reached it.

7 You can go wherever you want and learn all kinds of secrets.

'You' because it starts with a capital letter.

If students have problems, point out that some of the words here are already arranged in phrases: wherever you want / all kinds of secrets / You can go.

8 reading

9 (1) reading (2) rocket (3) noise / roar (4) silence (5) imagination (6) future (7) places (8) Robinson Crusoe's (9) moon (10) stories

Rhyme and alliteration

Rhyme

a) line 9 b) no (time / climb)

c) line 11

Ask if these sounds are spelt the same. Yes – beach / reach.

d) did / hid (lines 13–15)

Alliteration

line 8: *past* and *present* line 11: *rocket* and *reach* line 12: *Camelot* and *Crusoe*

Discussion

1 an encyclopaedia
2 Within the last fifty years – the first men landed on the moon on 20th July 1969.
3 line 2: try line 3: space line 4: place line 6: race

Space Thought

Vocabulary work

1 a) spacecraft b) aircraft, hovercraft
2 a) urge (line 2) b) ceaseless (line 2)
3 A squabble is used to describe a quarrel which is about something very unimportant. The writer is suggesting that people quarrel about unimportant things while there are great human problems to solve.

Understanding

1 an astronaut – a traveller in a spacecraft
2 Not certain. Words like: 'wonder why', 'while', 'stare you in the face'.
3 Likely answers: war, famine, disease, poverty, illiteracy and lack of education.

Alliteration

'p' – planet, place, problems

Does reading really matter?

Vocabulary work

Paragraph 1

1 a) latest (line 9) b) these days (line 3)
2 a quick, brief look

Note that a 'glance' is the opposite of a 'stare' (line 5 of 'Space Thought'). The short time it takes to look at a photograph contrasts with the longer time it takes to read about something.

Paragraph 2

3 a) accurate (line 14) b) wonderful (line 13)
4 a) exact (line 26) b) nothing (line 23)

Paragraph 3

5 a) maybe (line 30) b) watching (line 33)
c) requires (line 35)

Paragraph 4

6 a) in other parts of the world (lines 49–50).

If necessary give a hint: the phrase is six words long.

b) subjects (line 46) c) community (line 49)
d) just (line 43) e) want (line 48)

7 You hold it tightly. 'Gripping' here means exciting.

Explain that 'grip' / 'gripping' is commonly used in this sense, eg: I was gripped by the film.

Paragraph 5

8 a) thus (line 51) b) moreover (line 54)
c) essential (line 51)
9 a) more (lines 56 and 59)
b) better (lines 57 and 58)
10 swimming, cooking, writing
11 Examples:
a) Hard work is the secret of success. / We could not find the secret drawer in the desk, though we looked all over for it.
b) Smoking is a very bad habit because it can cause serious illness. / My sister has an annoying habit of always losing her pen and wanting to borrow mine.

Prefixes

a) unimportant b) inaccurate
c) uninteresting d) misunderstand
e) inessential f) inexact
g) disadvantages

Understanding

1 a) Disagrees – 'Reading is … essential' (line 51)

b) Agrees – 'the latest news is brought to us hourly' (lines 9–10)

c) Agrees – 'an encyclopaedia … is always better for good illustrations.' (lines 16–18)

d) Agrees – 'we also need words' (lines 18–19)

e) Disagrees – photographs do give 'a very good impression' (lines 21–22) of an elephant's appearance, although they cannot give other types of information.

f) Disagrees – 'in the same way' refers back to the pattern of paragraph 2 where good points of photos are mentioned and are compared to writing. Here the writer states the positive points of good films: 'action, movement, colour and … music' before mentioning how books can be an even better experience. (lines 28–30)

g) Agrees – 'reading a novel requires imagination' (lines 34–35)

h) Agrees – 'some important events happen when there are no cameras around' (lines 39–41)

i) Agrees – 'a newspaper does not just report the news' (lines 42–43)

j) Agrees – 'Read at least a little every day.' (lines 60–61)

2 No, he likes them, but he wants us to understand that reading has advantages that these other forms of communication lack.

3 a) Fiction – writing about something which is not true, such as a story; non-fiction – writing which is based on fact, such as in history or science books, a biography or autobiography.

b) 1 novel – fiction

2 encyclopaedia – non-fiction

3 newspapers – non-fiction

Pronouns

a) reading (line 1)

b) a photograph (line 20)

c) elephants (line 24)

d) a newspaper (line 42)

e) reading (line 55)

Paragraphing

1 a) 'Some people', who think reading is not now important. (line 1)

b) Paragraph 2 explains why photographs cannot replace writing.

Paragraph 3 explains why reading a novel can still be enjoyable.

Paragraph 4 explains why we still need newspapers.

2 'thus' (line 51)

Punctuation

Note that commas before 'and', indicated (,) below, are optional.

1 My uncle visited Washington, Boston(,) and New York on his visit to the United States.

2 The United Kingdom consists of England, Wales, Scotland(,) and Northern Ireland.

3 We bought lettuce, tomatoes, cabbage(,) and oranges at the market.

Spelling

paragraph 1: radio, novel, latest

paragraph 2: wonderful, accurate, nervous, illustrations, elephant, tells

paragraph 3: excellent, imagination, differently

paragraph 4: gripping, cameras, around, happening, interesting, community

paragraph 5: essential, human, habit, little

UNIT 6

The world's most popular game

How it all started

Vocabulary work

Paragraph 1

1 a) ancient (line 1)
b) injured (line 9)

Check students understand the restricted use of 'ancient' – see Unit 1, Vocabulary, page 8.

2 a period of one hundred years

3 a) particular / special
b) sure. Examples: I am certain John can swim. / Margaret is certain to come.

4 banned (line 11)

5 b) dangerous

Paragraph 2

6 a) game
b) a match / game between different countries
c) They are the same colour or design.
d) a small piece of wood with a special substance at one end that catches fire when rubbed sharply along a strip on a matchbox

7 standard (line 19)

8 a) a group of people who are interested in the same thing, eg a sport or a hobby (such as photography)
b) a piece of wood used as a weapon; a stick with a special head used in a sport like golf

Ask what two different meanings 'a golf club' could have – a group of people who play golf together, or the stick used to hit a golf ball.

9 worldwide (line 24)

Paragraph 4

10 'un' (unpopular)

11 d) not being used

12 an extra wheel carried in a car in case there is a puncture

Ask if students know what 'spare time' means – leisure time.

13 a famous person from the entertainment world, like an actor, singer or sportsman/woman

Ask for guesses why this word is used – perhaps because a star shines brightly in the sky, and similarly a famous person stands out from the crowd.

14 Originally the word meant a person who owned a million pounds or dollars. It now often means just an extremely rich person.

15 undoubtedly (line 48)

16 a) have a great hope / desire / wish
b) something imagined while asleep. Example: Last night I dreamed I was a butterfly.

Understanding

1 a) False – the first sentence does not mention towns. Towns are mentioned in reference to the later English customs.
b) True – people were injured. (line 9)
c) False – it developed in the early nineteenth century. (lines 14–15)
d) False – the cup awarded in 1871 was for the best English club. (lines 20–21)
e) True – 'a year later' than 1871. (line 23)
f) False – 'the ball could be picked up and carried' (line 28)

In fact, in American football there is no goalkeeper. In the form of football played in the rest of the world, the ball can be handled only by the goalkeeper.

g) True (lines 38–40)

2 c) the fourteenth century

3 So that clubs could play against one another.

4 A game in which a group of people play together. Some common team games: volleyball, basketball, baseball, rugby (another type of football game), hockey, cricket. Some non-team sports and games: tennis (though in doubles two players make a 'team'), swimming, diving, athletics, such as running and jumping (however, relay races are run by teams).

5 Formal – they are played by strict rules.

This might be a good opportunity to explain the useful and necessary distinction between formal and informal letters / speech / writing / behaviour / dress.

6 Because it gives them an opportunity to become rich. (line 44)

7 explanatory

Ask students the meanings of each type:

- **explanatory (noun: explanation) – writing which explains what something is, writing such as we find for example in an encyclopaedia (though an encyclopaedia will generally contain much biographical writing as well);**
- **biographical (noun: biography) – writing which tells about someone's life;**
- **autobiographical (noun: autobiography) – writing which is a person's life story told by him / herself;**
- **narrative (noun: narrative) – a story.**

Paragraph organisation

1 Paragraph 1 tells of the earlier history of football, before the nineteenth century when it was informal, with no agreed rules. Paragraph 2 tells of the history of the game in the nineteenth century, when rules were established for the game.

2 American football

3 Why football is the most popular game in the world.

Spelling

beggar	doctor
calendar	grammar
father	cellar
ruler	mirror
adviser*	publisher
similar	refrigerator

*** advisor is used in American English (and sometimes in British English)**

The greatest in the world?

Vocabulary work

Paragraph 1

1 believe (line 7)

2 of all time (line 9)

Paragraph 2

3 have the same job as his father

4 a person who knows a lot about a certain subject

5 he / she stops working

6 surprisingly

Paragraph 3

7 a) quick-witted (line 37)
b) joy (line 46)
c) moreover (line 44)
d) courageous (line 37)
e) constantly (line 39)
f) certainly (line 34)
g) accurately (line 41)
h) enthusiasm (line 45)
i) effective (line 42)

Give examples of how to use 'effective' – an effective cure for an illness / an effective air-conditioning system / an effective teacher.

Paragraph 4

8 a) modest (line 51)
   b) poor (line 58)

9 someone who plays on your team

10 Example: My greatest ambition is to become a doctor / a great singer / a good swimmer.

Understanding

1 a) False – 'Pele's mother did not want him to follow in his father's footsteps' (lines 13–15) because his father had been poor and often injured when playing football.
   b) True (line 49)
   c) True (lines 59–60)

2 Pele could 'head' the ball as skilfully as he could kick it.

3 The reasons are given in lines 50–59.

Note that Pele's skill as a player, detailed in paragraph 3, is not really a reason – he is a role model because of his personal qualities.

4 biographical

5 The question mark suggests that Pele may be the greatest star, but this is not certain and there may be differing views on this.

Ask what word or phrase in the first paragraph also suggests this idea: 'Many people believe ...' (line 7). Ask why it may not be certain. Because footballers have individual qualities and skills; they play in different places and at different times. It is difficult to compare accurately a current player with a past player.

Idioms

1 – c 2 – b 3 – d 4 – e 5 – a

Paragraph organisation

1 (1) Pele's true name (2) When he was born (3) Where he was born (4) Where he was given his nickname (5) He does not know *why* he was given it (6) That he does not know *what* it means (7) He became world famous when young ('soon' – line 6) (8) Many people believe Pele was the greatest footballer of all time.

2 c) Pele's career

3 paragraph 3 – Pele's skill as a footballer
   paragraph 4 – Pele's character

Treasure houses of knowledge

Describing the world

Vocabulary

With regard to 'pence' (line 16), you may also want to point out that now 'pence' is used as both singular and plural (one pence, two pence, etc.) but that before 1971 the pound sterling contained 240 pence / pennies, and the singular form of 'pence' then was penny.

You can discuss the illustrations of 'icon' at this point, or leave them until later, perhaps after the Vocabulary work. Invite students who are familiar with computers to explain these icons used in creating documents or examining them. The first icon is used to create a new folder (where several documents on the same subject can be kept); the scissors is used to delete text; the third is used to create a new document; the magnifying glass enlarges text displayed on the screen; letter *I* changes letters into *italic*. Students may be able to suggest other icons.

Vocabulary work

Paragraph 1

1 a) chance (line 10)
b) special (line 8)
c) often (line 8)
d) rich (line 1)
e) find (line 10)
f) searching (line 7)
g) topic (line 8)

2 a) generally

Paragraph 2

3 a) best-known (line 11)
b) latest (line 19)

Paragraph 3

4 pictures (not only photographs – illustrations would include photographs and drawings)

5 an excellent encyclopaedia – 'excellent' is a stronger word than 'very good'

Paragraph 4

6 a) a complete change of method
b) especially

Paragraph 5

7 expensive (line 42)

8 d) immense

9 store (line 43)

Paragraph 6

10 update (line 55)

Paragraph 7

11 a hand-held device for moving the cursor without keying

Ask if students know what a cursor is. If the word is new, they can probably work it out from the context – a flashing pointer on the screen that can be moved around the screen by the mouse to highlight text or icons.

12 d) connected with the topic

13 very quickly

Paragraph 8

14 A person who is physically or mentally unable to act like other people, eg a person who is blind or deaf or unable to walk.

Paragraph 9

15 a) pictures
b) writing

Understanding

The passage is not difficult, but warn students to take particular care when answering these questions. They must read them carefully and answer only on the basis of what the passage says.

1 a) True (lines 8–10)

b) True (line 12)

c) False – text says best *known* – not the best (line 11). It may be the best in many people's opinion, but students are asked to answer *according to the passage*. The writer of the passage does not give his / her opinion.

d) False – see answer to (c) above.

e) True – they cost only a few pence. (lines 15–16)

f) False – the passage says 'some' (line 27), not 'all', of the shorter encyclopaedias are written specially for young people.

g) True – '*not only* printed on paper' (lines 32–33), makes it clear encyclopaedias are still available in book form.

h) False – they are cheaper. (line 41)

i) False – they are certainly useful for handicapped people, but the passage does not say they were invented *specially* for them.

j) False – the passage does not say they are more expensive (they may be, but the passage does not say so).

k) False – we see both text and images. (lines 81–85)

2 This is a metaphor. The author suggests that knowledge is very valuable, as are the precious metals (such as gold and silver) and jewels that would be kept in a treasure house.

3 It was first published in the eighteenth century. It was published every week. Because each part was short, the price was low, so many more people could afford to buy them.

4 'latest edition' (line 19)

5 A small bird found mainly in tropical countries (around the equator), 10–100 centimetres long, usually with beautiful, brightly coloured plumage (feathers). Parrots live in trees, and in captivity can imitate human speech.

6 The number of years since 1986.

7 b) New facts are being found out.

Discussion

The *main* disadvantage of encyclopaedias on disc is that computers are expensive and most of them are not portable. Try to elicit other reasons by questioning: Do you think text and pictures are better quality in a book or on a screen? What about just browsing through an encyclopaedia as suggested in the first paragraph? Might this be easier and more pleasant with a book? ('Browse' is a useful word, which originally described only how an animal feeds on leaves, but is now also used to describe a person looking through a book, newspaper or magazine in a casual way.) Do you like to look at books in an armchair? How must you usually sit when you are working at a computer?

Pronouns

1 just to turn over the pages. (lines 8–9)

Remind students that pronouns usually refer to nouns, but may refer to phrases, as used here.

2 weekly part(s) (line 14)

3 The *Encyclopaedia Britannica* (line 17)

4 other excellent shorter encyclopaedias (lines 24–25)

5 CD discs (line 44)

6 multi-media encyclopaedias (lines 79–80)

7 parrot (line 83)

Paragraph organisation

1 The first two sentences tell us what an encyclopaedia is. The third sentence tells us about the two ways we can use encyclopaedias – for finding specific information or for just browsing through.

2 c) its size

3 Two reasons might be suggested: (1) the writer wants to emphasise how much information an encyclopaedia may contain and (2) because later, in paragraphs 4–9, he is concerned with encyclopaedias on disc that are used on a computer and which are very small and convenient. He wants to stress the contrast.

4 Shorter encyclopaedias

5 Encyclopaedias on discs

6 paragraph 5: Discs are cheaper to make, store and transport.

paragraph 6: Discs are cheaper to update.

paragraph 7: Discs are more 'user friendly' – easier to use.

paragraph 8: Discs are better for the handicapped.

paragraph 9: Multi-media CDs also convey movement and sound.

7 a) Paragraph 3 would go best with paragraph 2 because paragraph 3 simply extends the topic of paragraph 2 – encyclopaedias in general. On the other hand, paragraph 4 introduces a completely new topic – encyclopaedias on disc.

b) Paragraph 8 would go best with paragraph 7 because paragraph 8 extends the topic of paragraph 7: how 'user-friendly' discs are. Ask which two words at the beginning of paragraph 8 make this clear and serve to join it to paragraph 7: 'particularly useful' (line 71). Paragraph 9 introduces a new and more developed kind of disc, the multi-media disc.

Spelling

reliable	probable
visible	capable
agreeable	flexible
terrible	fashionable
comfortable	incredible
avoidable	noticeable
horrible	valuable
sensible	edible
responsible	miserable
lovable*	indescribable

*** Point out that 'lovable' drops the final 'e' of 'love', but 'noticeable' keeps the final 'e' of 'notice'.**

A closer look

Vocabulary work

Paragraph 1

1 a) sometimes (line 4)

b) deep (line 5)

Paragraph 2

2 a) very frightening. (Stress that 'terrifying' is much stronger than 'frightening.)

b) enormous. (Mention that 'large' or even 'very large' would not be as strong.)

c) thrown violently. (Point out that 'hurled' is a stronger word than 'thrown' – it suggests more force – hence 'violently'.)

d) great / tremendous / immense

3 A bomb is a weapon used in war. It contains explosive material. Bombs can be dropped by aircraft.

4 Houses and buildings are the most obvious answers here, but anything 'material' (that can be owned) would be a suitable answer.

5 b) to calculate with some care and knowledge

Paragraph 3

6 a round, flat article used for holding food

7 all the time

If necessary give letters as clues until someone comes up with the right answer.

8 Examples: I'm so thirsty – can you squeeze some oranges, please? / There are six people in our family, and our car is very small, but we usually all squeeze into it.

9 occur (line 25)

Paragraph 4

10 a) completely (line 39)

b) famous (line 31)

11 one that no longer exists, such as a dinosaur

12 sailors who live on the island

Paragraph 5

13 broken suddenly and violently into many pieces

14 a very strong and sudden current of air, such as is caused by an explosion, eg of a bomb

Paragraph 6

15 a) weather

b) The lava has been changed by the weather – wind and rain.

16 a) Fertiliser is something which is added to soil to make crops grow better.

b) 'Fertile' means able to produce crops.

Ask for the word of opposite meaning, to describe land which cannot bear crops – 'barren'.

17 b) advise

Understanding

1 centuries

2 250,000

3 The lava is being compared to a stream or river. The movement is therefore like a river – strong and continuous.

Note expressions such as: The crowd streamed out of the cinema. / A stream of traffic moved steadily along the highway.

4 A lighthouse is used to warn sailors of dangers, such as rocks. A lighthouse is usually in the form of a tower, so that the light can shine out high over the land or water.

5 The volcano on Stromboli is active all the time.

6 The quotation marks suggest that this is not really a firework show (which would be something made by man), but a volcano.

Check that students understand what fireworks are. Ask if they remember fireworks being mentioned in any other unit (ie Unit 4, page 32, line 26 and Vocabulary section, page 33).

7 Mount Everest is the highest mountain on earth. Therefore this stresses the great height of the cloud.

8 a) Stromboli and Krakatoa

b) The volcano on Stromboli is small, but always active. It attracts tourists and acts as a lighthouse. It is a good / friendly volcano. On the other hand, Krakatoa was an extremely destructive volcano, killing 36,000 people (line 50).

9 That volcanoes should have the benefits listed in the last paragraph.

10 The use of volcanoes for heating homes. We would have been able to sink pipes deep into the earth to obtain the hot water only recently.

11 In some volcanic areas there are hot springs where people may bathe. These contain substances such as sulphur which can help people suffering from certain illnesses.

12 On Stromboli the volcano is a tourist attraction and acts as a lighthouse for local sailors.

Paragraphing

1 This first paragraph tells us what a volcano is. It *defines* the word 'volcano'. It might be found in a dictionary. (Suggest students look up 'volcano' in their own dictionaries.)

2 The first sentence. (Ask how the other sentences develop the topic sentence – they show how a volcano is terrifying.)

3 a) Some volcanoes are under the land and others are under the oceans.

b) Most are where the 'plates' meet, and molten rock is squeezed up when they move; others occur where plates are weak and the lava bursts through.

c) How many volcanoes are there? – about 800

4 In each paragraph, the first sentence. (You can explore how each paragraph expands upon these first sentences.)

Punctuation

Note that five commas are optional. These are placed in brackets.

We very rarely see the beginning of a new volcano. In Mexico(,) in 1943, some villagers saw a crack appear in a field. Smoke gushed out(,) and the crack became wider. Ash and rocks were hurled high in the air(,) and then red hot lava poured out. After a week(,) a 150m high volcano had grown. Mount Paricutin, as the volcano is now called, grew to 275 metres in a year(,) and 410 metres after nine years.

Spelling

a) rough
b) cough
c) right
d) fight
e) daughter
f) laugh
g) sleigh
h) bough
i) light
j) eight and eighteen

Other examples: weight, neighbour, frighten, plough, trough, might

The day a mountain exploded

A city frozen in time

Pre-reading discussion

Before the lesson you might like to ask students to find out from an encyclopaedia what they can about the Roman Empire. This should help them answer question 2, and also give them some useful background knowledge. The following *basic* facts are useful. Rome was founded about 500 BC. It grew in size and importance and over a period of about 500 years became the capital of a great empire that stretched (west to east) from Spain to Iran, and (north to south) from Britain and Germany to North Africa. Tunisia, Egypt, Syria, Jordan, for example, were all part of this empire. Eventually it was invaded by other nations from the north and east, and Rome itself was captured in 500 AD.

2 d) 2000

3 Italy

Understanding the map

These questions may be answered before or after the passage is read.

1 a) north

b) west

c) north

d) south

2 Naples

3 Surrentum

4 Herculaneum

You could ask further questions based on the map requiring use of reference books before the next lesson, for example: (1) What are the names of the three large islands on the small map? – north to south: Corsica, part of France; Sardinia and Sicily, part of Italy. (2) What is the country in the south-west corner? – Tunisia. (3) What is the sea called? – the Mediterranean.

Vocabulary work

Paragraph 1

1 'Towered' suggests comparison to a tower, therefore it stresses height. (Example: Though Jack was only 16, he towered above his father.)

Paragraph 2

2 a) leapt (line 9)

b) immense (line 9)

3 'Terrifying' is a much stronger word than 'frightening'.

4 One that can kill you.

Check if students know 'poison' (noun) – something you eat, drink or inhale that can kill you.

5 choked / suffocated. (They both mean unable to breathe.)

6 b) a very small number

You might like to teach / revise the difference between 'few' and 'a few':

Barbara has a few interests outside school.

Here 'a few' means several and indicates that she has more than one. This is a *positive* remark.

Barbara has few interests outside school.

In this sentence 'few' means very few, hardly any. This is a *negative* remark.

Paragraph 3

7 b) like no other

Paragraph 4

8 amusing / funny

Draw students' attention to the spellings of 'humour'/ 'humorous' (the 'u' is dropped in the latter).

9 handsome, good-looking

Explain that 'handsome' is used to describe a man and 'beautiful' a woman. A woman may also be described as 'handsome', but we rarely use 'beautiful' to describe a man.

Understanding

1 a) True – it is described as a port (line 2). If students look at the map, they will see that Pompeii is not now on the sea – the flowing lava poured into the sea and extended the coastline.

b) True – the mountain is described as peaceful. (lines 5 and 10)

c) False – we are told it was buried until the eighteenth century (line 21). If a new city had been built over it, then it would not have been possible to excavate the city as fully as has been done.

d) False – everyday items are listed in lines 33–34. (Students may of course argue that these items are valuable to us now as they help us to understand ancient Rome and its empire.)

e) False – thousands of people died. (line 17)

f) False – we are not told whether the paintings are portraits (pictures of people). (line 37)

g) False – the poem, for example, is certainly not amusing. (lines 48–50)

h) False – we are told that he / she was writing about 'human life' in general (line 47). It is also clear from lines 1–8 that no one knew this mountain was in fact a volcano.

i) False – before the ruins were discovered, they were protected by being buried under stone and ash (lines 20–21). The archaeologists simply discovered the ruins (lines 21–24).

2 The contrast is with the quite unexpected eruption.

3 An open question – students might suggest items of clothing, books, pens, furniture, TV sets, computers.

4 Boxers – as boxing is the most violent combat sport we now have. Wrestling, karate, judo are also combat sports, but much less violent than boxing.

Discussion could develop on the students' views on the merits of combat sports, particularly boxing.

5 The remark is amusing because it contradicts itself. The writer himself had to write on a wall to write this remark.

Spelling

paragraph 1:	kilometres	beautiful
paragraph 2:	restaurants	terrifying
	poisonous	thousands
	choked	buried
	eighteenth	archaeologists
paragraph 3:	because	unique
	daily	amphitheatres
	museums	sandals
	pottery	
paragraph 4:	personal	ordinary
	humorous	

Paragraph organisation

By this stage, students should be familiar with paragraphing, but this article is particularly useful to remind students, if necessary, that:

- **a paragraph does not need to have a single topic sentence, particularly if the paragraph is a short one. It should, however, be on one main topic. The first paragraph illustrates this well. The paragraph gives information about the size and location of Pompeii, but neither of the two sentences in this short paragraph can be said to be the topic sentence;**
- **when a paragraph does have a topic sentence, it is often the first sentence, as in paragraphs 3 and 4. But the topic sentence may come later, for example in paragraph 2 it is the fourth sentence.**

Paragraph 1

Pompeii was a large city and a port.

Paragraphs 2–4

paragraph 2: Suddenly there was an immense explosion.

paragraph 3: Because the destruction was so sudden, the ruins of Pompeii give us a unique picture of what daily life was like in a Roman city nearly two thousand years ago.

paragraph 4: On the walls of many houses we can see not only beautiful paintings, but also read many personal messages written by ordinary people.

Photo, page 70

1 water; in shallow streams

2 someone who is travelling on foot

Picture, page 72

1 Papyrus was made from a tall water plant like a reed.

2 b) is the best answer. The picture would suggest that the lady was able to write (and we know from other sources that in fact some Roman ladies were taught to read and write). But this does not mean that all women were able to do so or that husbands in general encouraged their wives to do so.

What Pliny remembered

Vocabulary work

Paragraph 1

1 noticed (line 1)

2 to stop rain falling on you

Paragraph 2

3 a) after a very short time

Ask if students know a phrase which means the same as 'immediately' – right away.

4 save

Paragraph 3

5 d) to move unsteadily. (This suggests the buildings were shaking, but not actually falling.)

6 fled (line 14)

Be sure students understand this is the past tense of the verb 'flee' – the past participle is also 'fled'. The verb is very commonly used about people running away from a disaster.

7 a) wailing (line 15)

b) shrieking (line 15)

8 very young children

Paragraph 4

9 d) a sort of yellow

Explain that '-ish' can be attached in a similar way to most colours, eg reddish, bluish, greenish.

Paragraph 5

10 shore (line 23)

11 You place it in / push it into the water.

12 calm (used in line 24 to describe a person)

Ask: **a) What is the *opposite* of calm if describing a person? – excited**

b) What word means the same as calm if describing the sea? – smooth

13 fell down

Understanding

1 a) False – he was a young man at the time of the events. He wrote 'later' (last line of the introduction).

b) True – see 'she' (line 9), 'her' (line 9), 'her' (line 23).

c) False – she sent a message (line 8). If she had come, she would not have needed to be rescued.

d) False – she lived at the foot of Vesuvius. (lines 8–9)

e) True (lines 7 and 9). However his first intention was just to have 'a closer view' (line 7) of the eruption, but when he got Rectina's message, he decided to try to rescue her. Later it seems he might have tried to help another friend. (lines 23–24)

f) False – the ash is said to be *like* snow. (line 18)

g) False – the uncle was always calm. (line 24)

h) False – he had sailed on to visit / rescue another friend at Stabiae. (line 23)

i) False – Pliny was not there when his uncle died – the servant told him later what happened. (line 29)

2 soil and ashes (lines 4–5)

3 a) the distance between Misenum and Mount Vesuvius

b) the wind was blowing southwards from Vesuvius to Pompeii, and it would have carried the sound away. We are told about the wind on page 68, line 14.

4 a) to observe the eruption

b) to rescue Rectina

5 They were probably afraid of being crushed by the houses if they fell.

6 To protect his face from hot ashes and so that he would not breathe in ashes or poisonous gas.

7 We are not told – probably because he could no longer breathe.

8 He went to rescue Rectina (line 9) and then his friend at Stabiae (line 23). He always acted calmly (line 24).

Paragraphing

paragraph 1: c) Vesuvius erupts
paragraph 2: b) My uncle departs
paragraph 3: d) The escape from Misenum
paragraph 5: a) My uncle's last days

Possible titles for paragraph 4: The return home / The following day. (Note the third sentence acts as the topic sentence.)

Pronouns

1 Pliny's uncle
2 the cloud
3 Pliny and his family
4 Pliny's uncle
5 Rectina's
6 Pliny
7 Pliny

Punctuation

2 Mount Vesuvius has erupted over one hundred times since it destroyed Pompeii in AD 79. The two most serious eruptions were in 1631, when 3000 people were killed, and in 1944. In this last eruption no one was killed, but great damage was done. The volcano will almost certainly erupt again. The two million people who live in Naples live in constant danger.

Note that points (as used for full stops to mark the end of sentences) may be used to follow the letters A.D. as these are abbreviations (for the Latin *anno domini*, in the year of the Lord), but the modern practice is not to use them. See Basic punctuation guide, page 91, section 2.

Spelling

paragraph 1: umbrella, unusual, height
paragraph 2: immediately, received, rescue
paragraph 3: buildings, shrieking
paragraph 5: friend, calm, launched, sulphur

Discussion and writing

is, was, is, are

Fresh water to drink

Digging for water

Pre-reading discussion

2 The water may be polluted; only a small amount can be drawn at a time; it has to be carried in containers perhaps long distances and there is the danger, particularly for small children, of drowning.

3 Danger in digging wells: the walls may fall in. (Students will probably not mention the danger from gas unless they have already read the story. Do *not* suggest this now – let the story retain its surprise.) Danger in use: children especially (but also adults and animals) may fall down uncovered wells.

Part 1

Vocabulary work and understanding

1 a) 1 lift

'Heave' is here used as a noun, but it is more commonly used as a verb. Explain that 'heave' suggests that the lifting is done with difficulty: you heave a heavy box; your chest heaves after you have run a distance. Laura's father has to lift his body just with his hands.

b) 3 exchanged

2 to mark out where he was going to dig the well

3 in case they got hurt – their father was throwing soil out. (Note that 'in case they drowned' would not be the right answer, as he had not yet reached the water level.)

4 He held it very tightly.

5 a) about 3 metres

b) The depth must be greater than Mr Ingall's height (his head was below the ground), but shallow enough for him to jump up and heave himself out.

6 a horse

7 a) He shot it – 'he took his gun'. (line 10)

b) So that there would be enough meat to eat / it would taste good.

8 a) 2 Pa starts the well

Remind students that the title must reflect the *main* topic of the section – the other topics *support* this main topic.

Part 2

Vocabulary work and understanding

1 a) 2 strong

b) 2 went down quickly

Be sure students understand that 'slid' is the past tense of 'slide' and that the past participle is also 'slid'. Sliding is a smooth movement – you slide on ice, for example. Here Mr Scott goes down by letting the rope pass between his hands.

c) 3 pulled

Explain that 'hauled' suggests pulling with difficulty, because the buckets are heavy: Fishermen haul in their nets when they are full of fish.

d) 3 looked with eyes half closed

e) 1 intended

2 d) at least twice the depth. There is a bucket at each end of the rope. When one bucket is fully down, there is rope reaching from it up to the windlass, and enough rope round the windlass to let the other bucket reach down to the bottom when the first bucket is wound up. (The rope wound round the windlass can be seen in the picture on page 79.)

3 Because her father says: 'Better be safe than sorry.'

Ask if students know another English proverb with this meaning – 'Look before you leap'. Point out that sayings often contradict one another. One saying offering opposite advice to these two proverbs is: 'He who hesitates is lost.' Students usually find proverbs interesting. Are there similar proverbs / pairs of proverbs in the students' own language?

4 A windlass is a device for winding in a rope or cable. Some sort of load will be at the end of the rope – here a bucket.

5 c) Work on the well continues (The windlass would be a good title only for the first paragraph. Laura peeping into the well is certainly not the main incident.)

Part 3

Dictionary definition of 'keel'

You might want to take the opportunity of revising some of the dictionary study in Unit 2. In Some dictionary entries, page 19, there are nine types of information listed which a dictionary may give other than for spelling and meaning. Ask which of these nine are provided here. Elicit: pronunciation (using phonetic alphabet – i: represents the long 'ee' sound), parts of speech, help with grammar (check if students remember what 'nc' means – noun, countable, so we know 'keel' can be used in the plural. Ask for some common nouns that cannot be so used, eg equipment, furniture, luggage). Ask if any types of information are inapplicable for this word – syllable and stress (as 'keel' has only one syllable); formal / informal; different forms of verb. Example sentences are probably not necessary. Views may differ on need for languages of origin and illustrations.

Vocabulary work and understanding

1 a) 2 dawn. (Explain 'sunup' is more used in American English than British English.)
   b) 1 squeak
   c) 2 bent low

2 a) He was happy with how the work was going.
   b) He guessed that Mr Scott had fainted because he did not reply when Pa shouted to him.

3 to help Mr Scott

4 in case he got into danger

5 when we are cold or frightened

6 c) It was sunny and she had to stop the sun shining into her eyes so she could see into the well. (The well was dark inside, but if the sun had not been shining, she would not have needed to shade her eyes to see into it.)

7 a bird

Explain if necessary to students that 'meadow' means a field of grass. This question provides an opportunity to revise / teach the names of some common birds.

8 d) she was frightened

Part 4

Vocabulary work and understanding

1 a) it was tight

2 Mr Ingalls was holding the other end and his wife was not strong enough to lift him.

3 Mr Ingalls had to climb up the rope.

4 Mr and Mrs Ingalls turned the windlass together and the two of them were strong enough to pull up Mr Scott.

5 bucket (more commonly used than 'pail')

6 with difficulty (because it was so heavy)

7 To give her husband a drink, or maybe bathe his forehead with a cloth dampened in the water.

8 He was only partly conscious.

9 a) bother (line 84)

b) found out (line 84)

10 To see whether there was any poisonous gas in the well. If there were poisonous gas, the candle flame would go out.

11 c) not clear

12 The baby moves on hands and knees.

Ask what 'crawling' suggests here about the way the spark was moving – slowly. We often say traffic crawls at rush hours – when there is too much traffic on the road.

13 b) to make the well safe (by exploding the gas)

Part 5

Vocabulary work and understanding

1 slapped (line 112)

Ask what sort of a hit a slap is – with the flat of the hand. Ask what sort of a hit is one with the fist, such as a boxer might make – a punch.

2 a) hauled (line 118)

Ask, what 'hauled' suggests about how something is carried or moved – with effort, difficulty. Note 'haul' appeared in question 1c on page 80 with the sense of 'pull'.

b) stale (line 119)

We say also that old bread is stale, but old (spoilt) meat and vegetables are bad / rotten.

3 sound sent back, such as that of your own voice on top of a hill, or in a large room

Elicit: 'echoing' is the present participle of 'echo' used as a verb.

4 Mr Ingalls had been in great danger from the flooding water, yet he had bothered to save his spade.

5 Mr Scott said that the water came in more quickly than he could pull Mr Ingalls out. (line 111)

6 Laura could see herself and the sky reflected in the water.

7 in case they fell down the well

8 Cold water would be very pleasant to drink in hot weather.

9 The bucket was full to the top – so that some was spilling over the top.

Making a well

How to make a well: spade; two – one to dig and one to haul up buckets of earth; circle; the grass inside the circle; dig down until you reach the water; a windlass; to haul up buckets of earth; two buckets; people take it in turns to dig and to haul up buckets of earth; walls collapsing, poisonous gas which cannot be seen or smelt, and water / quicksand; put a lighted candle in a bucket and lower it down the shaft, or tie gunpowder (wrapped in cloth) to a piece of string, light it and lower it down to make the gas explode; a platform and a heavy lid for the hole; to stop things falling into the well, including people.

Spelling

simple	uncle	tunnel
personal	towel	travel
vowel	apple	quarrel
electrical	gentle	label
hospital	paddle	model
practical	capital	

Sweet enough to drink

Vocabulary

You can further explain:

- borehole (line 5): We often use 'bore' (as both verb and noun) in a different sense: The film bored me. / John is a great bore; he always talks about the same thing. Ask what these sentences mean.
- plaster (line 25): You could ask: What different meaning does plaster have when we speak of a plaster / a sticking plaster? – a piece of cloth that is stuck to the skin to cover a wound. Ask which meaning students think is more useful for a student of English to learn first. There may be a difference of opinion here, but sticking plaster is likely to be considered the more common and useful meaning.
- fibreglass (line 27): A fibre means a very fine, hair-like thread of a substance – wood and cotton are made of fibres. Fibreglass is a modern material, made of fine fibres of glass woven together and coated with plastic to make a smooth surface. Baths, shower trays and small boats are now often made of fibreglass.

Vocabulary work

1 a) a device for making fresh water from salty water
 b) sal (as in salt)
2 a) very important
 b) minor
3 c) dependable – that you can be certain will work without problems

This is a common and useful word: point out useful phrases such as a reliable car, a reliable person, a reliable newspaper report.

4 water brought in by a truck.

Explain that a truck is a road vehicle for carrying goods; 'lorry' has the same meaning. A truck / lorry (or ship) that carries liquid such as water or petrol is called a tanker.

5 to do with the sun. (Solar power is power produced by the sun.)
6 a) local: to do with a particular place
 b) made by people who live in the area

Elicit that 'developed' suggests changed in some way. The local people did not invent the idea of the desalinator, but they adapted it to suit local needs and materials and made it themselves.

7 a) leather
 b) Example: Scientists are always looking for new cures for dangerous diseases.
8 The bowl used for washing in the bathroom is called a washbasin. Small basins are used in the kitchen for mixing food or for carrying food to the table.
9 A liquid evaporates when it turns into vapour.
10 A vapour condenses when it turns into a liquid.

Understanding

1 Because the water is often too salty to drink.
2 for example (line 4)
3 The two most obvious and important advantages: it is cheaper and it produces salt. Further possible advantages: people do not have to carry water from the trucks which may not stop near their homes; people can be quite sure the water is pure.
4 So that the heat generated by the sun cannot escape.

Ask if students know the useful related word 'watertight'.

5 Black absorbs the heat from the sun, so the water heats and evaporates more quickly.
6 It would be quicker and easier to build, if you had the materials and skilled workers. A fibreglass desalinator could be easily moved to a new place if necessary as it would be in one piece.

7 Fibreglass basins are more expensive. They need special materials not always available locally, and also workmen with special skills.

8 a) when scraping off the salt

b) impurities would get into the salt

9 For a family – it does not produce enough water for a village.

10 a) in the summer

b) it is hotter

11 In less than two and a half years you have saved enough money to pay for the fibreglass desalinator by not having to buy trucked-in water. / In less than two and a half years you have saved enough money by not having to buy trucked-in water to pay for the fibreglass desalinator.

12 a) the brick and plaster basic type

b) it costs less to build

Desalinator drawing

1 d 2 e 3 b 4 a 5 f 6 g 7 c

2 No – if the cover were flat, drops of fresh water would fall back into the salty water in the basin.

3 the bottom of the basin

Paragraphing / Connecting sentences / Pronouns

1 The first sentence in each paragraph

2 a) the cost – paragraph 5

b) how it works – paragraph 3

c) how it is made and how much it can produce – paragraph 4

3 a) for example (line 4)

b) however (line 6)

c) therefore (line 7)

4 a) now (line 9)

Elicit how 'now' makes a contrast. The first paragraph states the problem, but *now* there is a possible solution to it.

b) the desalinator

5 basin

Elicit that the first sentence tells us that the main part of the desalinator is the basin (line 17). The second sentence tells us how this basin (line 19) is used to evaporate salty water.

6 a) the basin

b) fibreglass / a basin made of fibreglass (both answers equally possible)

English Reading and Comprehension

Teacher's Book 2

Contents

UNIT 1

Crime fighters!

A clever way to catch a thief

Pre-reading discussion

1 Explain 'detective' – a person whose job is to find criminals or get information. You can take a vote on who likes watching films about crime and detectives. Encourage students to talk about any films they have seen.

2 Examples: scientific tests to identify and match fibres (threads of material), hair and blood, or to identify dead people through dental records, fingerprinting.

Make sure 'fingerprinting' is elicited, eg ask students how police know who has touched something, but do not go into detail about this, or mention DNA or voiceprints as these are dealt with later.

3 Ask for the meaning of 'ingenious': clever at making or doing things especially in a new way. If not known, students may be able to work the meaning out from the context by considering how the use of 'also' refers back to 'clever' in the previous point. Ask them to check in their dictionaries – this is a good opportunity to remind students of the importance of dictionaries.

Vocabulary work

1 a) poor
b) light
c) left
d) bottom
e) quietly
f) guilty
g) dirty

You could ask for the opposite of 'right' when used in the sense of being correct (wrong) and take the opportunity to remind students that many English words have more than one meaning.

2 a) unlocked, unsurprised, unafraid
b) You may ask students first what suitable 'un-' / 'in-' / 'dis-' words they know, then to hunt in their dictionaries to find more, eg able / unable, armed / unarmed (spelling note: only one 'n', unless 'un-' is added to a word beginning with 'n' like natural / unnatural); definite / indefinite, accurate / inaccurate; and advantage / disadvantage, agree / disagree (spelling note: only one 's', unless 'dis-' is added to a word beginning with 's' like satisfied / dissatisfied. Elicit that not all words beginning 'un-' /'in-' / 'dis-' are part of such pairs, eg uncle / infant / distance.

3 careless / carelessly

4 a) centre
b) afraid

5 d) absolutely dark. (Point out that the context makes it clear which meaning 'quite' has – the servants had to feel their way.)

6 a) bird
b) hen

This might be an opportunity for revising / teaching the names of some common animals, including the names for the sounds they make (see 'crow' in line 12): eg dogs bark, lions roar, sheep bleat, bulls bellow, cats miaow, cows low or moo, bees hum, birds cheep / twitter, ducks quack.

7 It must be something that marks fingers – this would suggest a powder. Soot is the black powder found in fireplaces and chimneys.

Understanding

1 a) 4 so that the thieves could not come in. (Note that at this point he did not know a servant was involved – only when the thefts continued did he know the thief must be someone in the house.)
 b) 3 more things were stolen
 c) 1 because no one from outside could come in
 d) 3 to go into the room singly
 e) 3 a table with a box on it covered with soot
 f) 3 only the thief had no soot on his finger

2 He had servants and valuable things (line 1) which were taken from his house.

3 So that the servants would not see the soot on the top of the box. If they had seen it they might have guessed the trick. The darkness also added to the sense of mystery.

4 They had been told that the cock would crow when the thief put his hand on the box and no cock had crowed.

5 No – people nowadays would not believe in a magic cock.

6 Even if the rich man had beaten the thief, he might not have confessed. Moreover, someone who was not the thief might have wrongly confessed, just to stop the beating. This method was more ingenious and more certain.

Paragraphing

paragraph 1: b) Some mysterious thefts!
paragraph 2: d) The rich man explains his plan
paragraph 3: c) The servants must obey
paragraph 4: a) The thief discovered

Pronouns

a) the rich man
b) the thief
c) some of the servants
d) the thief

Spelling

taking	called
middle	magic
happen	innocent
listened	carefully
very	covered

As good as signing your name

Vocabulary work

Paragraph 1

1 b) a long narrow raised part on a surface
2 c) individual
3 a) ends
 b) A tip can also mean (1) a piece of advice: Our teacher has given us some good tips on how to revise for our examinations; (2) a sum of money given, for example to a waiter or taxi driver, as a reward.
4 maybe (line 4)

Paragraph 2

5 a) two children born to the same mother at the same time
 b) identical twins look exactly the same
6 a) exactly (line 10)
 b) further (line 11)
 c) discovered (line 11)
 d) classified (line 16)
 e) therefore (line 16)
 f) task (line 20)

Paragraphs 3 and 4

7 permitted (line 28)

8 a) very valuable

Point out that though 'in-' as a prefix usually makes the sense negative (see also Vocabulary work, question 2, page 5), 'invaluable' is an exception. Two other exceptions are 'inflammable', which means the same as 'flammable' – easily able to burn, and 'innumerable' – too many to count.

Paragraph 5

9 a small room in a prison

10 c) the only one of its kind. (You may want to point out that in informal English 'unique' is often used to mean rare, but that this is not really correct.)

11 a) specimens (line 44)

b) scene (line 47)

c) analysed (line 49)

12 suspect (line 53)

Teach if necessary 'suspect' (verb) and 'suspicion' (noun). Note the different stress: sus<u>pect</u> (verb) and <u>sus</u>pect (noun).

13 composition (line 38)

14 a) that they are the same colour or design – that is they 'go' with one another: The skirt and blouse were a good match.

b) a game, such as a football match; a small stick with chemicals on the tip we rub along a surface to make fire

Paragraph 6

15 a) individual (line 57)

b) laboratory (line 59)

c) method (line 59)

Understanding

1 a) True (lines 5–6)

b) False (lines 9–11)

c) False – 'only in the 1880s ...' (line 8). (In fact, the first criminal was caught by using fingerprints in 1901.)

d) False – they are used in crime prevention and to identify murder and accident victims. (lines 21–22)

e) False – blood from any part of the body can be used.

f) False – we are told that the method is not yet perfect (line 59), ie it cannot be used with the same degree of certainty as traditional fingerprinting and DNA testing. But even if it became as reliable, it would be used in different circumstances. So voiceprints would not *replace* fingerprints.

2 cups, saucers, plates, jugs, bowls

Check if students know the collective name for these items – crockery; and for knives, forks, spoons – cutlery.

3 that fingerprints are unique

Stress that in over a hundred years of fingerprinting none of the millions of fingerprints taken has ever been found to be identical to another. Before this discovery people could see fingerprints were different, but they did not know for certain that they were unique.

4 a) You write it.

b) See the Basic punctuation guide, section 7(c), page 88. Here the apostrophes are used because the thumb prints are not real signatures like *written* names.

5 Because they cannot write.

Ask if students know what we call someone who cannot read and write – illiterate. Illiteracy is not being able to read or write. Ask what the words of opposite meaning are – literate / literacy.

6 thousands of years ago (lines 4–5)

7 matching two sets of fingerprints to see if they have been made by the same person

8 Yes – because the checking must be done immediately. We have been told (lines 18–19) that otherwise matching takes a long time.

9 discovering crime; paragraph 2: the 'scene of a crime' (line 17)

10 Because it is stopping crime taking place. Here it would probably be a bank robbery.

11 a) DNA testing involves testing cells from the body, as found for example in blood and hair. Fingerprinting involves taking impressions from the ridges on the fingertips.

b) 'Fingerprinting' has been applied to DNA testing because it has a *similar* aim – to identify people. Both fingerprints and DNA are unique.

12 'Print' is taken from 'fingerprint' because the characteristics of the voice are being used to identify a person in the same way as the characteristics of the shape of fingerprints can be used.

13 No, because the guilty person was the one who had *not* marked his finger. Moreover, the rich man did not make the servants press their fingers on paper to make a print, etc.

Paragraphing

1 The second and third sentences give two different *examples / illustrations* of how man has used the special nature of fingerprints. The first is of potters in the past, the second of illiterate people even nowadays.

2 d) using fingerprints to detect crime. (The other topics support this main topic.)

3 the first sentences of each paragraph

You can show how in each paragraph the later sentences develop and illustrate these topic sentences.

Pronouns and possessive adjectives

a) someone (line 23) – trying to get into a bank

b) unknown innocent people (line 31)

c) each person (lines 38–39)

d) people (line 54)

Punctuation

1 When we touch something, we leave a little sweat from ridges in our fingertips. This is what makes a fingerprint.

2 The British police started using fingerprints to catch criminals in 1901, and soon police all over the world were doing the same. The FBI (Federal Bureau of Investigation in the United States) now holds records of over 100 million people.

3 On each fingertip is a pattern of ridges. These ridges enlarge the area of skin. Therefore there are more nerve endings than if the skin were smooth. This is why we have such a great sense of touch in our fingertips.

4 a) How do the police take someone's fingerprints?

They ask the person to first place his/her fingers on a pad which has ink on it and then press the fingers on a sheet of paper.

b) Sometimes a person leaves very clear fingerprints, for example if he has dirt or blood on his finger. Sometimes fingerprints cannot be seen. What does a policeman do to make the fingerprints visible?

He places a special powder on the object (such as a pane of glass) where he believes there may be a fingerprint, and this makes the fingerprints visible.

c) How can a criminal be sure he does not leave any fingerprints?

He wears gloves.

The Olympic Games

The most important thing …

Pre-reading discussion

Students may already know a lot about the Olympic Games. Accept information, but avoid giving information they will be reading about.

Vocabulary work

Paragraph 1

1 countries

Paragraph 2

2 events (line 12) or sports (line 18)

Paragraph 3

3 modern (line1)

4 a) foot (line 21)

b) nearly (line 22)

5 a large piece of flat open land

You could ask what part of speech 'plain' is here (noun) and what other meanings 'plain' has when used as an adjective, eg a plain piece of paper – one without writing on it; a plain-looking person – someone who is not good looking; a plain meal – a simple one.

Paragraph 4

6 female

7 a) a vehicle with two wheels, pulled by horses (illustration on page 13), used for racing and in battle in ancient times

b) money paid to the government

c) taxi; taxis are cars which can be hired with a driver

8 awards (line 37)

Paragraph 5

9 a) raise it

b) lower

10 a) very / extremely large or immense

b) shown

11 a) pigeon (line 47)

b) trumpet (line 45)

c) stadium (line 49)

12 a stick with material at one end that is burnt to give a light

Understanding

1 a) False – 'every four years... *except* during the two World Wars' (lines 2–4)

b) True – 'meet peacefully ... better' (lines 7–8)

c) False – 'in the 1896 games ... the competitors were all men' (lines 10–11)

d) True – 'more and more sports have been included' (lines 17–18)

e) True – 'number of nations ... greatly increased' (lines 16–17)

f) False – 'The games continued ... in the same place' (lines 24–25)

g) False – a number of sports such as running in armour and horse and chariot racing are no longer included. (lines 30–34)

h) False – 'a *special type* of fighting which was a *mixture* of wrestling, boxing and kicking ...'. Modern boxing and wrestling are two very different sports. (lines 30–32)

i) True (lines 50–54)

j) False – the passage says *most* important; winning is of course still important. (lines 59–60)

2 1940 and 1944. (The dates are World War I: 1914–1918; World War II: 1939–1945.)

Note that students can answer this question without knowing the dates of either war if they notice the closeness of two of the three dates. It would be interesting to check how they reached their answers.

3 Because Athens is the capital of Greece, where the first Olympic Games were held (line 22).

4 In wrestling you grab hold of your opponent and throw him. In boxing you punch your opponent with your fists.

5 a) metal, such as steel; to protect the body
b) Because armour is so heavy.
c) No – because soldiers no longer wear armour.

6 Women would be killed if they watched the games.

7 Differences: number and range of contests is now wider; no longer held in one place; the events are now not only watched by spectators on the site, but all over the world via TV, and by both men and women; since 1900 women have taken part, too; these days people of all nations (not just one) take part; rather than having a single prize for the single winner of an olive wreath, gold, silver and bronze medals are now given for first, second and third places; rather than receiving rewards of good jobs and tax allowances, today's winners may get financial rewards from sponsorship and by becoming professionals at their sport; in the last century the Olympic Games were cancelled in periods of war rather than peace being declared while the games occurred.

Similarities: held every four years; contests of skill and strength; winners become famous and have great prestige.

Paragraph organisation

1 a) When were the first modern Olympic Games held?
The first modern Olympic Games were held in 1896.
b) How often are the Games held?
The Games are held every four years.
c) When and why were they cancelled?
They were cancelled during the two World Wars.
d) What is the purpose of the Games?
To give people of different countries the opportunity to take part in athletic contests and also to get to know each other better.

2 b) Developments in the Olympic Games. (Note that the other topics support this main idea.)

3 a) Where were the ancient Olympic Games held?
They were held on the plain of Olympia, at the foot of Mount Kronos, in southern Greece.
b) When did the Olympic Games start?
They started in 776 BC.
c) How often were the Games held?
They were held every four years.
d) How long did the Games continue?
They continued until AD 394 (for 1170 years).

4 b) Contests and competitors in the ancient games. (The other topics support this one.)

5 b) That the most important thing is to take part.

There may be more than one view here, and many students may think that the opening ceremony is the main topic. Ask them why they think this – probably because most of the paragraph is devoted

to describing it. Ask why (b) might be the right answer – because 'But perhaps what we should remember *most* ...' (lines 55–56) and also the title of the article strongly suggest this. Elicit that the description of the elaborate opening ceremony is there to make a contrast with the humbler real objective of the games – just to take part. The fact that the inspiring words are displayed with the names and countries of the winners also emphasises this contrast. Note that very important information often comes at the end of an article because that is what we remember most when we have finished reading.

Punctuation

1 The Hungarian Karoly Takacs lost the use of his right hand in an accident. He taught himself to shoot with his left hand, and he won gold medals for shooting in both 1948 and 1952.

2 The Olympic flag shows five rings. Each ring represents one of the inhabited continents. Each ring is a different colour. The flag of every nation taking part in the games has at least one of these colours in it. The rings are joined together to represent friendship between nations.

Finding out / Discussion

1,2 Answers will depend on when this book is studied, but the 2000 games were held in Sydney. 199 countries took part. Most medals were won by athletes from the United States. The 2004 games will be in Athens.

If students cannot easily access information, you might like to invite them to guess, rather than just telling them the answers. You could give them the correct figures in the following table plus two others of your choice for each entry so they can choose an answer. Be sure they understand that a sport may have more than one event, eg there are running races for different distances.

Olympic Games 2000
Countries: 199
Sports: 28
Events: 300
Athletes: 10651

Ask if they think there were more men athletes than women – yes.

Ask roughly what proportion they think were women – 40% (4069 women / 6582 men).

3 a) The Olympics bring many visitors who will spend a lot of money.

b) The cities usually have to build places for the sports to take place, and places for the athletes to live. The cities have to be sure there is enough transport to take people to the stadiums and hotels for them to stay in.

4 The most common winter sports are skiing, skating, bobsleighing and ice hockey.

Spelling

four	people
nations	thirteen
increasingly	ancient
southern	thousand
continued	special
armour	chariots
wreath	speeches
sound	hoisted
pigeons	balloons
released	stadium
brought	throughout
appear	countries

The marathon

Pre-reading discussion

Some dictionary entries may also give the figurative meaning 'a lengthy journey or task'. If so, explain that this expression is not very common and at the intermediate stage students are perhaps best advised not to use it. However, if examples are needed: It was a marathon journey to cross the mountains on foot. / We had the marathon task of looking for the letter in all the drawers in the office.

Vocabulary

Paragraph 1

1 a) famous (line 4)
b) attempted (line 5)
c) defeated (line 7)
d) delivered (line 12)

2 a) old
b) bad

3 c) as soon as

Paragraph 2

4 c) remarkable action

5 b) about the same length

6 a) to cause people to remember (an event or dead person)
b) comMEMORate (suggests 'memory').

Stress how you can often guess the meaning of an unknown word in this way.

7 A shepherd looks after sheep.

Ask what someone who looks after goats would be called – a goatherd. Check also 'herd' – a group of animals, especially used for cattle and sheep.

8 something that is given or received for work or services, or to show gratitude. Examples: A reward of £10,000 was offered by the bank for information about the robbery. / John's father gave him a new bicycle as a reward for passing his examinations.

Paragraph 3

9 a) liked by many people. Example: Emma is popular with everyone, she is always so cheerful and helpful.
b) extremely tired. Example: Paul was quite exhausted after climbing the mountain in only three hours.
c) prevented from taking part in something, or from being given a prize. Example: Andrew was disqualified from taking part in the children's swimming competition because he was just one month too old.

10 a) staggered (line 33)
b) stumbled (line 31)
c) sympathetic (line 32)
d) particularly (line 28)

11 presented (line 41)

Paragraph 4

12 a) only
b) finishes

Understanding

1 a) False – the date is 400 BC (line 4) so the battle was fought about 2400 years ago.
b) True – they defeated the Persian army. (lines 6–7)
c) False – he died and we are not told how, but he could not have run if he had been wounded. He probably died because of exhaustion: 'He ran without stopping' (line 11).
d) False – we are not told that Spyridon Louis had been a soldier. Philippides had been a soldier (line 8).
e) False – he was given a cup (line 40). The gold medal was given to an American runner. (lines 35–37)
f) True – 'popular … with both sexes'. (lines 43–44)

g) False – four pieces of information support this answer: 'many thousands of people take part' (lines 49–50); 'many … just for fun' (lines 52–53); an annual event (line 48); in London (line 48).

h) False – '*some* competitors are serious athletes, but …' (lines 51–55)

i) False – *many* do (lines 52–53), but the passage does not say everyone collects money for charity.

2 Greece

3 Because Spyridon was Greek (therefore a fellow-countryman) and Greece had won no other event.

4 England

5 Phillipides' great run from the battle at Marathon to Athens.

6 d) modest

You might like to check that students understand the meaning of this and the other words in the list, and then they can use them in sentences.

Discussion

2 a) He was disqualified because he was helped by spectators.

5 **Before attempting the questions, look at the photograph on page 21. Ask what the young man is doing and what his disability may be. Elicit that he has no legs, and he is taking part in a disabled sports race. Ask if they can read and interpret what is written above his number – Atlanta is a city in the United States; the Olympic and Paralympic Games were held there in 1996. Ask for further information about the Paralympic Games – events for disabled people held every four years after the Olympic Games. In 2000 at Sydney over 4000 contestants took part from 123 countries.**

The paragraph on the Paralympic Games would not go well with the article on page 18 but might be included in the article on page 13, between paragraphs 4 and 5.

Paragraph organisation

There could be some discussion here. Some students may feel that the first sentence of the first paragraph is the topic sentence. But the main topic is the Battle of Marathon – the source of the race's name. Similarly some students may feel that the first sentence of the third paragraph is the topic sentence – but the main topic of the paragraph is the 1908 race.

paragraph 1: 'It takes its name from a famous battle of long ago.' (second sentence)

paragraph 2: 'When the Olympic Games … with a race of similar length.' (first sentence)

paragraph 3: 'The race held in 1908 … is particularly famous.' (second sentence)

paragraph 4: 'One of the most popular marathons … in London.' (third sentence)

Pronouns

a) a Persian army (line 5)

b) Philippides (line 8)

c) Spyridon Louis (line 19)

d) Dorato Pietri (line 30)

Drawing with light

A new art form?

Pre-reading discussion

1 Ask students to look carefully at the photograph and say where they think it was taken. Elicit that it was taken in a park and that the setting looks like a country in Europe or the United States – it was taken in London. Ask about the man on the left. Elicit that he is taking photographs; he is a professional photographer. Ask about the cart, eg Why are there photographs fastened to the front of the cart? / Are they there to advertise the photographer's work? Elicit also that the cart is where the photographer can develop his photographs; the chair is there for people to sit on and be photographed; that the camera the man is using is different from one we might use today – it is much larger and it is on a support / stand. If the name of the stand is not known, wait until the passage is read for the answer. Discuss how the clothing is different from modern day – the lady is wearing a long dress, a short cape and a hat. The men are wearing bowler hats and have sideburns – short hair growing down below each ear. Ask for the name of what the child is sitting in – a pram / pushchair.

Ask them to make a guess when, *roughly*, this photograph was taken. You may take a vote using the five dates suggested. Do not give them the answer (1888). When they have read the passage, ask what clues there are: The photograph must have been taken after 1826, when photography was invented; photography has now developed, for people can be photographed in parks, with exposures shorter than the eight hours of the first photograph (line 17), but the camera was still heavy and needed a tripod (lines 20–24). We learn that the first amateur hand-held camera was invented in 1888 – but such cameras did not replace the heavy professional ones. So 1888 or 1901 would be the most likely dates.

Vocabulary work

Paragraph 1

1 b) do not consider as unusual

2 a) 1 imagine only with difficulty

b) Examples: (1) We could hardly see the house / words on the page / sign, etc. because it was so dark. (2) We could hardly move in the bus / room / lift / car because it was so crowded. (3) Paul could hardly breathe or move because the water was so cold / he was so frightened.

3 photographs

Paragraph 2

4 many developments (lines 18–19)

5 a) but

b) necessary

6 equipment (line 25)

7 dear / costing a lot of money

Paragraph 3

8 round

9 a) an easily remembered expression advertising something: slogan (line 34)

b) (to do with) a person who does something for pleasure not money: amateur (line 36)

Ask what the opposite of amateur is – professional. Mention that these terms are much used in sport and entertainment – professional players / musicians / actors are paid for taking part; amateurs are not.

10 'Mass' suggests that very many people were beginning to take their own photographs.

Paragraphs 4 and 5

11 have enough money

12 a) stimulated (line 48)

b) accurately (line 51)

Understanding

1 a) True – 'we now take photography very much for granted'. (lines 1–2)

b) False – they use photography daily. (lines 6–7)

c) False – *less* than two hundred years ago (lines 10–11)

d) False – note the Kodak slogan: '... we do the rest'. (line 35)

e) False – 'nearly everyone can afford ...' (lines 38–39). (Some students may rightly say that many poorer people cannot afford a camera, but the question specifically states 'according to the writer'.)

f) False – photography has stimulated ... painting. (lines 48–49)

2 Examples: scientists may take / use photographs, eg of laboratory experiments, animals, plants, the stars, for study purposes, etc. They often take photographs through a microscope. Doctors regularly use X-rays. The police take photographs of scenes of crime and fingerprints. They issue photographs of people they are searching for – criminals or (innocent) missing people.

3 a) the use of glass plates (line 22) instead of metal plates (line 16); the length of exposure times (lines 17 and 23)

b) Cameras were heavy. / Exposures were long and the camera had to be completely still while the shutter was open.

Ask students if they understand what a tripod is. If not, mention a triangle, or the prefix 'tri-'. Elicit 'three' and that a tripod is a three-legged stand such as is used by photographers to support their cameras, as in the photograph. Vocabulary may be extended to 'triple' (and the series 'single', 'double', etc.).

4 He used film (made of a sort of plastic) not glass plates. (Ask how this was an improvement – glass breaks easily and film was lighter than glass, so the cameras were lighter.) The roll of film was then sent away to be processed.

5 Example: You take the photographs and we will process them for you.

Which do students think better, the slogan or a version such as this, and why? The slogan is shorter and more memorable. 'Press the button' suggests a simple but maybe exciting action, and 'we do the rest' suggests that the customer is being looked after by someone he/she can trust.

6 a roll of film that has been used to take photographs and so exposed to the light

7 **Elicit that a society is a group of people. We use 'society' in two main senses: (1) a community, or people living together in a country under the same laws, etc.; (2) a club – a group of people interested in the same hobby or sport, eg a photography society. 'Social' is the adjective and is often used to describe relationships. Therefore a social occasion would be one when people come together in a friendly way, eg for a wedding or birthday party.**

8 a) richer people

b) they could afford to pay painters to paint portraits of themselves and their families.

9 When photography was first invented.

10 Example: Before photography was invented, painting was used to record what people and places looked like. Photography can now do this quickly and cheaply. Therefore painters are free to paint in different and more imaginative ways.

11 the nineteenth and twentieth centuries

Paragraph organisation

1 d) The different uses of photography today

Point out how the other topics illustrate these various uses. Topic (d) includes all of them.

2 c) Early developments in photography

Point out how the other topics give examples of the developments.

3 Paragraph 3 deals with the beginning of amateur photography. Paragraph 4 deals with amateur photography today.

Take this opportunity of reminding students that sometimes a part of an article may be written *equally correctly* as one, two or maybe more paragraphs. The golden rule is simply that there must be *unity* in the paragraph – each paragraph must be about one topic.

4 Photography and painting

5 No – because the topics are quite different. They are not related as are the topics of paragraphs 3 and 4.

Spelling

a) camera

b) amateur

Note 'amateur' can be pronounced a - ma - ter or a - ma - cher ('ch' as in chicken)

c) photographer; painter

d)

teacher	professor	helicopter
meter / metre*	triangular	farmer
spectator	sailor	soldier
inspector	emperor	theatre
familiar	hotter	character
author	litre*	data
lawyer	lava	
baker	similar	caterpillar
cellar	manager	area

*** A 'metre' is a measure of length in the metric system (American spelling of this length is 'meter' – see also 'liter'); otherwise a meter means an instrument for measuring something passing through it eg water/electricity meter.**

How to take better pictures

Vocabulary work

Introduction

1 take photographs; photographs

Original meanings come from firing a gun at a person or animal: The hunter shot the rabbit. / We could hear rifle shots. Ask how 'shoot' / 'shot' is used about football: We lost the game, but our captain made some fine shots. / Owen shoots, but fails to score!

2 a) Examples: The game was so exciting – there was no score until the very last minute! / I was very excited when I opened my present. / There was great excitement as they waited to know who had won first prize.

b) Example: We rushed to the window when we heard the police-car sirens.

3 hoped for (line 7)

4 disappointed (line 4)

5 a) the teachers

b) She works for the magazine.

Lines 1–12

6 'Grip' means to hold very tightly.

7 a) together

b) roughly / firmly

8 a) compose (line 5)

b) centre (line 7)

9 Example: I squeezed all the juice out of the oranges.

10 Example: We closed the shutters to keep out the strong sunlight.

11 the border of wood put round a picture when you want to display it

Lines 13–30

12 natural

13 when they don't know you are doing it (line 18)

14 illuminate (line 20)

15 abilities

Understanding

1 The exposed film is treated in a special way to produce photographs.

2 Because he /she is excited to see what the photographs will look like.

3 Moving the camera when you are taking a photograph. / It makes the photographs blurred (not sharp).

4 Go nearer to your subject.

5 You did not take care when looking through the viewfinder – you pointed the camera too high.

6 You did not take care when looking through the viewfinder – your sister was standing right in front of the tree and close to it.

7 In a very stiff manner, as though they were statues carved (made) from wood.

8 If you stare into the sun, you screw up your eyes.

9 a) The flash on most cameras is not strong enough to illuminate subjects beyond three metres.

People's eyes may appear red on a photograph taken with a flash if they have looked straight at the camera.

b) We can learn to take better photographs by reading books. We may be able to borrow them from a library.

Punctuation

a) Why are people's eyes sometimes red on photographs taken with a flash? The reason is simple. The pupil of the eye opens wide in the dark. The flash goes off too quickly for the pupil to close. The flash illuminates the blood vessels at the back of the eye. This is what we see on the photograph.

Check if students know the two meanings of 'pupil': (1) a schoolchild (It can also be used of an older person being taught, but then 'student' is the more common word.) (2) the black centre of the eye that expands and contracts to control the amount of light entering the eye

b) What can be done about 'red eye'? Some cameras have a white light which shines onto the subject as soon as the shutter button is lightly pressed. This makes the subject's pupils close down. The photographer presses the button further to set off the flash and take the photograph.

(There might be a paragraph break here.)

Another method is to have two flashes a fraction of a second apart. The subject's pupils close when the first flash goes off and the photograph is taken with the second flash.

UNIT 4

A land apart

Introducing Switzerland

Pre-reading discussion

Encourage as many students as possible to offer ideas and opinions, but do not offer information at this stage. If a student says something obviously wrong, rather than directly saying he / she is wrong, ask 'Are you sure? What do other people think?' The passage contains much information on Switzerland and you do not want to anticipate this.

Vocabulary work

1 countries (line 3), lands (line 7)

2 b) However

Point out that 'however' is generally marked off with a comma (two if it is not the first word in the sentence) but a comma is not placed after 'yet' (which must always be the first word).

3 a) prosperous (line 7)
b) perhaps (line 8)
c) picturesque (line 15)

Warn students this word describes only places (old, traditional scenes, especially), not people. A girl / woman might be described as good looking, pretty or beautiful, a boy / man as good looking or handsome.

d) wonderful (line 13)
e) tourists (line 17)
f) famous (line 10)

4 b) cover a large area

5 a) fertile (line 14)
b) varied (line 7)
c) major (line 20)
d) textiles (line 25)

Check what kinds of textiles students know – cotton, wool, silk, nylon, etc.

e) renowned (line 25)
f) skills (line 26)
g) international (line 27)

6 cameras, microscopes, telescopes, binoculars, lenses of all kinds, including spectacles

Explain that 'optical' means to do with the eye or light. A person who makes and sells spectacles is an optician.

7 the main offices

8 Example: George is very proud of his brother, who has just won the swimming championship.

9 ensured (line 37)

10 not assisting either side in a war

11 b) in addition

12 a) on the other hand

13 a) occur (line 54)
b) assistance (line 53)
c) maintains (line 40)

Ask students to look up 'maintain' in their dictionaries. Elicit / explain that 'maintain' has the sense of keeping in good condition / providing with the means to live: A car should be maintained in good condition. / It is hard to maintain a family properly on a low income. The other common meaning of 'maintain' is to claim to be true: The driver maintained that he had not been driving fast when the accident happened.

14 b) sent without delay

15 a) human
b) to do with acting as a human being should do – having qualities of kindness and mercy. Humanitarian aid is help, such as food, housing and medical supplies for people who are ill, wounded, or homeless.

Understanding

1 a) False – '*one* of the smallest' (lines 2–3)
b) True – as France is twelve times larger than Switzerland, and Italy only seven times larger. (lines 3–5)
c) False – 'perhaps … for most' so not *everyone* goes mainly to see the Alps (lines 8–9). See also 'equally attractive … many people … lakes' (lines 11–16).
d) False – the passage mentions only an army and an air force (line 41). In fact, Switzerland is surrounded by other countries. It has no coastline.
e) False – there is no Swiss language, but three major languages spoken in different areas.
f) True – see the first sentence of paragraph 5.
g) False – 'since 1815' (line 39)
h) True – because that war was fought after 1815. (line 39)
i) False – the floods and earthquakes (lines 54–55) are not said to be in Switzerland. Help is sent to other parts of the world.

Explain that earthquakes never occur in Switzerland. There are often floods, however – elicit why – if winter snows melt too quickly in spring, or if in summer there is unexpectedly heavy rainfall, the water can pour off the mountains more quickly than streams and rivers can take it away.

j) True (lines 52–55)

2 The languages mentioned in paragraph 4 suggest Germany, France and Italy as the major ones. Austria (where German is the national language) is a fourth, and Liechtenstein (a very tiny country, area 160 square kilometres, population 31,000) is the fifth country.

3 a) snow and ice
b) Skiing and skating are the most obvious; bobsleighing and tobogganing are others.

4 in case it is invaded

5 Switzerland is kept apart from other countries by the mountains. It is also 'apart' in the political sense of being traditionally neutral and not a member of the UN.

Check that students understand 'apart' – away from. Ask if they know the prepositional phrase 'apart from' meaning except / except for: Everyone in the class went on the visit except / except for / apart from Lewis.

Paragraphing

1 a) size (41,293 square kilometres); one of Europe's smallest countries; one seventh the size of Italy; one twelfth the size of France; varied landscape; prosperous
b) one of most beautiful European countries

Students do not always find it easy to distinguish a fact from an opinion. Discussion of this question should help. The answers for (a) are facts because everyone agrees they are true. The answer for (b) is based on personal preference.

2 a) the second paragraph develops the idea of beauty and variety
b) The attractions of Switzerland

3 d) trade and industry in Switzerland – the other topics are all aspects of this.

Note that tourism is considered an industry: 'the tourist industry'.

4 The languages of Switzerland / Languages spoken in Switzerland

5 neutrality. ('Independence' may be suggested – the word is mentioned in the first sentence of the paragraph, but it means simply that one country is not controlled by another. The paragraph goes further and stresses the country's neutrality, which has enabled it to carry out its humanitarian role.)

6 independence (lines 35 and 36)

Spelling

1 Europe, twelfth, beautiful, prosperous, picturesque, equipment, language, neutral, headquarters, earthquakes

2 a) business
b) peaceful
c) independence
d) crescent
e) immediate

Understanding statistics

Understanding

1 1 population: a) lowest – Jordan
b) highest – USA
2 land area: a) lowest – Belgium
b) highest – Russia
3 population density: a) lowest – Australia
b) highest – Holland

2 a) Switzerland
b) Holland
c) France
d) Austria

3 Italy, France, Egypt, UK

4 seven and a half

5 a) smaller; twice
b) third
c) the USA; Australia

6 Italy and UK

7 The Russian Federation

Discussion / Finding out

1 **The capital city of a country is usually the largest city. Is this true of the students' country? The population of Canberra is about one twelfth that of Sydney. Ask students to find out why this is so. You could also ask students to find out a) what the capital of Switzerland is (Bern) and if it is the largest city (No, Zurich is). b) Repeat the questions for the USA (Washington, not New York, which is the largest city).**

The first European settlement in Australia was in the south-east, around Sydney. This developed into a huge city. Up until 1901 Australia was composed of six separate (British) colonies. There was no capital for the whole of Australia. When it was decided to form a proper nation, there was disagreement about which city should become the capital: Sydney, or the next largest city, Melbourne. As a compromise a completely new city was built halfway between them at Canberra.

4 Australia is also a land apart because it is remote from Europe; there are great differences in animal and plant life from the rest of the world (eg kangaroo and duck-billed platypus); it is unusually large in area with a relatively small population; there are very few native people (the Aborigines); nearly all populated areas are around the coastline – the centre is mainly uninhabited desert.

Encourage use of encyclopaedias and other works of reference to gather information which can be shared in class.

William Tell and the apple

Vocabulary work

1 c) a long rounded piece of wood

2 a) You bend (your head or upper body) forwards to show respect or to acknowledge applause.

Ask who might bow in front of an audience – an artist after a concert. Elicit / teach 'applause' and 'acknowledge', both useful words.

b) the front part

Check students know 'bough' (same pronunciation) – the branch of a tree.

3 c) immediately

4 a) stride
b) To stride means to walk quickly with long steps: it suggests a sure, confident walk.

5 a) a bull
b) very loudly

6 a grip is a tight, firm hold. (See also Vocabulary work, point 6, page 27.)

7 a) free
b) a tight knot
c) This sentence illustrates the difference between 'lose' and 'loose': My brother is very forgetful. 'You would lose your head if it were loose!' my mother often tells him.

8 a) authority (line 23)
b) confident (line 25)
c) dares (line 22)
d) famous (line 27)
e) defy (line 23)

9 a) loudly (line 38)
b) good (line 33)
c) large (line 20) / great (line 37)
d) quiet (line 24) – not 'silent' (line 39) as this means making no sound at all
e) best (line 28)
f) nodded (line 32)

Be sure students understand that we can say 'nodded his head' or just 'nodded', but we must use 'head' with 'shake': He shook his head. 'He shook' would mean 'he shivered' or 'he trembled' – from cold or fear.

g) fail (line 37)

10 a) a curved band of all the colours (of the spectrum) that appears in the sky when the sun shines through mist or rain
b) It would be a knot with two loops.
c) A musician playing a violin or other stringed instruments makes a sound by drawing his bow across the strings.

11 a person who can shoot well

12 a) became
b) Example: My bag fell in the water, but the pool was not deep and I soon got it out.

13 a) furious (line 54). (Point out that 'furious' is stronger than 'angry'.)
b) split (line 51)
c) straight (line 50).

Point out how 'straight' is also used in line 11 and how it is often used in giving directions: Go straight ahead.

d) harmed (line 61)
e) instantly (line 63)

14 a) shouting loudly
b) approval / support / praise

15 hole

16 fasten the person or thing with ropes

17 a low continuous noise, not clearly heard, eg a murmur of conversation

18 there is heavy (a lot of) rain and strong winds

19 a) a number of people or things arranged in a line (eg a row of seats in a cinema, a row of desks in a classroom)
b) a quarrel

20 a) very tightly
b) past tense
c) cling

21 He succeeded in reaching the shore.

Point out 'succeed' must be followed by a preposition and gerund ('-ing' form) not by the infinitive.

22 the side of the lake

23 An old story which is not entirely true, but is probably based on true events that did happen and / or about a person who really lived.

Understanding

1 a) False – Gessler was cruel, but was not Swiss – 'foreign'. (line 2)
b) True – 'they would be instantly imprisoned' (line 8)
c) False – he asked William Tell who he was (lines 21–22). He had heard of him, however. (line 26)
d) True – 'murmur of anger' (lines 67–68)

e) False – he had the second arrow in case he missed the apple and hit his son – then he would fire it at Gessler. (lines 60–63)

f) False – Gessler did not make William Tell any promise about not sending him to prison. He only said William Tell would die if he failed.

2 The story does not directly say William Tell knew about the order, but it strongly suggests that he did, because it tells us he was proud and brave and 'simply strode' past the hat (lines 9–11). There must have been an announcement about this as Gessler wanted everyone to obey.

Students may suggest different answers. This is a good example of what a story may imply but not state openly.

3 By making William Tell fail a test of his ability as a marksman – Gessler hoped Tell would miss or even kill his own son.

Ask if students know what 'humiliate' means – cause to feel ashamed. Check if they know 'shame': a feeling of great unhappiness because of loss of self-respect; 'ashamed' means feeling inferior and / or guilty.

4 Because there was a storm and he would probably drown if he jumped overboard.

How the story is organised

section 1: b) Gessler's hat
section 2: d) William Tell refuses to bow
section 3: g) Gessler and William Tell meet
section 4: f) Gessler's game
section 5: e) William Tell accepts the challenge
section 6: h) The second arrow
section 7: a) The storm
section 8: c) William Tell and the apple – fact or fiction?

Discussion: suspense and surprise

1 a feeling of uncertainty about what will happen

2 Will William Tell hit the apple or hit his son – or miss both?

3 section 2: Will William Tell obey the soldier? What will the soldier do when he doesn't?

section 3: Will William Tell defy Gessler? What will Gessler do?

section 4: Will William Tell agree to shoot the apple?

section 5: Will William Tell hit the apple, or hit his son, or miss both? (the main point of suspense)

section 6: What will Gessler do now? What will Tell's answer be to the question about the second arrow? How will Gessler react?

section 7: Will Tell escape in the storm?

By answering these questions, students can revise the story line.

4 Perhaps William Tell's son's willingness to stand against the oak tree.

This is quite unexpected on a first reading. We are thinking only of Gessler and William Tell. But students may have different valid opinions. Encourage students to give opinions, even if you do not agree with them.

5 Because it shows how they are an independent and freedom-loving people.

Bravery: a discussion

1 **There may well be a difference of view here. There is obviously no clear and certain answer. You might like to take a vote before the discussion, then another vote after it. Stress that you should always be ready to change your mind if you have heard persuasive arguments on the other side or if you have simply thought about the matter longer. We admire the son's bravery in remaining calm and encouraging his father. What else might he have done? Cried, pleaded with Gessler, trembled or fallen on the floor. But the father had to keep calm too and concentrate on shooting the arrow accurately. Perhaps his fear of killing his own son was greater than the son's fear of being shot.**

UNIT 5

New sources of power

Renewable energy

Pre-reading discussion

1 Eliciting common uses of electricity will help greatly in vocabulary extension. When students have made their suggestions, ask how these could be organised into groups, under headings. A possible format to write on the board could be:

- lighting: in homes, public buildings (offices, hotels, banks, shops, schools, etc.), streets, sports stadiums
- domestic items: radio, TV, video, washing machine, iron, refrigerator, air conditioner, toaster, vacuum cleaner, polisher, cooker, food mixer, microwave oven, computer, etc.
- power outside home: TV / radio transmission, lifts, escalators, security devices
- transport: trains, trams, some cars (but petrol engine cars need electricity for ignition / lights)

Elicit that electricity is made by machines called dynamos. As dynamos turn, electricity is generated. Dynamos are turned by engines driven by oil, steam (using coal), or by turbines (engines driven by falling water, gas or the wind). This electricity can be sent to users by cable. Electricity can also be stored in batteries. Ask where we find batteries – radios, torches, cars, toys, etc.

2 by electricity or diesel engines; by steam.

Ask how the steam was produced – by heating water with wood or coal.

3 usually petrol or diesel fuel made from oil. (Some cars now have electric engines – they have batteries which have to be charged from the main supplies.)

4 The wind has driven windmills to grind corn, pump water, or drive machinery. Modern windmills are called wind turbines and they produce electricity.

5 a) They are natural elements so cost nothing and will last for ever.
b) They do not pollute the atmosphere.

6 There is information in the passages. Accept information volunteered by students, but do not elaborate.

Vocabulary work

Paragraph 1

1 used up

2 a) therefore (line 6)
b) need (line 1)
c) alternative (line 7)
d) now (line 8)
e) enormous (line 1)
f) calculate (line 5)
g) but (line 4)

Paragraph 2

3 a) convert (line 13)
b) equivalent (line 10)
c) showers (line 9)
d) cheaper (line 25)

4 a) use
b) the straps tied to a horse by which it pulls a vehicle
c) The writer is comparing the sun to a horse. Just as we can use the power of a horse by putting a harness on it, so we can use the power of the sun by using cells which produce electricity from its rays. This comparison makes the writing more interesting and vivid.

Paragraph 3

5 c) lasting for ever

6 to describe the part of a knife used for cutting, or the cutting part of a sword

7 a) pleasant to look at

Point out how the word is made from 'picture' – so a picturesque object is one which would make an attractive picture. See Vocabulary work, point 3c, page 31.

8 b) functioning well without much waste

Paragraph 4

9 great / enormous / huge

10 d) in great quantities

Paragraph 5

11 a) a wall built across a river to hold back the water, which raises the level of the upper part of the river and makes a lake or reservoir. (The force of the water can be used to drive turbines and make electricity.)

b) the wide mouth of a river into which the sea flows

12 When the tide comes towards the land, it 'flows'. When it goes away from the land it 'ebbs'.

13 a thick wire which carries electricity

Paragraph 6

14 a) 'Thermometer' is the most likely word. Some students may know 'thermostat', a device for controlling temperature. Insulated bottles for keeping liquids hot or cold are generally called thermos flasks (though 'thermos' is the name of a particular manufacturer).

b) geography / geology.

Elicit that 'geo-' signifies 'earth'.

c) 'Geothermal' must mean heat coming from the earth.

Understanding

1 a) True – 'this type of fuel will soon be exhausted' (lines 5–6)

b) True – '*now*' (line 8)

c) False – they convert light / sunlight. (line 13)

d) True – 'such methods cannot meet all our … demands' (lines 20–21)

e) True – 'wind ... inexhaustible source' (lines 26–27)

f) True – 'much more efficient' (line 31)

g) False – 'One wind machine … small town.' (lines 32–34)

h) True – wave stations are 'far out to sea' (line 47)

i) False – the cables take the electricity, not the waves. (lines 47–49)

j) False – this method can be used only 'in a few places' (lines 50–51)

2 To stress / emphasise these words. The writer is contrasting renewable sources with those that are going to become exhausted. He stresses that the need to find new sources is *urgent*.

3 a) verb

b) a light, short fall of rain; a device for washing yourself using a spray of water

c) He is comparing the fall of the sun's rays to rain.

d) That the sun sends its power in large amounts – also, perhaps, that it is a natural power. (Shower also suggests falling in a spray, over a wide area, as a shower in a bathroom does.)

4 a small player of tapes or CDs that you can carry around in your pocket

5 A dam because it would have many large turbines.

6 Because it stores the electricity in batteries. (lines 23–24)

7 Such photovoltaic cells are not yet powerful enough, and we do not yet have batteries large and cheap enough to store a large amount of electricity. (lines 23–25)

8 Because tides are certain – the height of tides varies but they always ebb and flow. The wind may drop completely.

Check if students understand 'reliable' – something that can be depended on: A reliable car is one that is not likely to break down, a reliable person can be trusted to do what is expected of him or her.

9 Because a wave power generating station has to be built out in the ocean.

Be sure students understand the difference between a tidal generating station, which can be built on the land, and which depends on tides, ie water coming towards and going away from the land, and wave generating stations, which must be built away from the shore where waves are high, and which depend on the motion of the waves rising and falling.

10 Because the source of energy (the hot rocks) is always there. It is a reliable source of power.

Paragraphing / Linking ideas

1 a) the first sentence

b) 'This power' repeats 'power' used in the first sentence and gives more information about it. (Ask for an alternative word for 'this power' here – it.)

c) The phrase 'this type of fuel' relates to 'coal and oil'.

d) 'Therefore' draws a conclusion from the information given in the previous sentences.

2 a) 1 The power that comes from the sun
2 the first sentence

b) this power (sentence 2) relates to the energy constantly showered on us by the sun (sentence 1).

c) The third sentence answers the question put in the second.

d) The fourth sentence gives more examples of objects that can be powered by photovoltaic cells – these are all small items we might be familiar with.

e) 'photovoltaic cells can convert sunlight into electricity' (lines 12–13)

f) 'but'

Ask if 'but' could go in the same place as 'however' – no, it would have to go at the beginning of the sentence.

3 a) paragraph 3: Wind power
paragraph 4: Hydro-electric power
paragraph 5: Tidal and wave power
paragraph 6: Geothermal power

b) Yes, the first sentences of each paragraph.

4 another

5 greater difficulties

6 Water is pumped underground, where hot rocks convert the water into steam.

7 then

Spelling

1 enormous, renewable, equivalent, buildings, supplying, calculators, scientists, inexhaustible, propeller, estuary, pumped, brought

2 radios, stereos

You can point out that some words ending in 'o' make a plural with 'es', and some with just 's'. There is no easy rule for students – newer English words just add 's', those longer in the language add 'es'. Examples of 'oes': potatoes, tomatoes, mosquitoes, volcanoes, heroes, echoes; examples of 'os': photos, radios, stereos, solos, pianos, studios, videos.

3 quantities, difficulties

The solar cooker – help for the developing world

Vocabulary

Paragraph 1

1 a) traditional (line 1)

b) **If students need prompting, you might suggest suitable openings of sentences, eg: In a traditional wedding in our country ...'**

2 a) ideal (line 2)

b) growth (line 5)

c) expensive (line 9)

Paragraph 2

3 escape

Paragraph 3

4 a) rotated (line 18)

b) adjusted (line 18)

c) focuses (line 16)

Point out that we use 'focus' in photography. To focus a camera means to make the photograph sharp. If a photograph is sharp, it is 'in focus' or 'well focused'. If it is blurred, it is 'badly focused' or 'out of focus'.

Understanding

1 Because trees grow again.

2 Black absorbs heat, so the cooker gets hotter and remains hot.

3 to direct the sun's rays / heat to a certain point, eg a hot plate

4 a building made of glass where plants can be grown

5 a) Foil means very thin sheets of a metal. Gold foil is used for decoration. Aluminium is a very light metal used for making aircraft and also pans used for cooking. Aluminium foil is therefore very thin sheets of aluminium.

b) It is used for wrapping food. It is sometimes called silver foil, because of its colour, though it is not made of silver.

6 So that the reflector can be moved always to face the sun as it moves in the sky.

7 a) the sun's rays

b) the glass cover

c) reflectors

8 a) the reflector

b) to move the reflector so that it is always at the right angle to the sun

c) the hot plate

d) a kettle

e) to heat water

Paragraphing

1 The shortage of wood for fuel in many parts of the world is the main problem. Other problems are: the distances women have to go to collect it, the growth of population, the high cost of kerosene and lack of electricity supply.

2 a) paragraph 2: Simple solar ovens in the ground

paragraph 3: Bowl-shaped reflector ovens

b) The last sentence of the first paragraph introduces the topic of both paragraphs – solar cookers.

3 'a more powerful cooker' (line 15)

Ask what phrase this contrasts with in the second paragraph – 'a simple solar oven' (line 11).

Discussion

a) Often people prefer traditional methods. They might prefer to roast food over an open fire. They might feel such food tastes better. A wood fire gives heat. A solar cooker cannot be used at night. They might feel having to move a bowl-type cooker around is too much trouble. Neither type is easy to make without tools, materials and skill – the bowl type is of course the more difficult.

b) Using gas, electricity or kerosene is much more convenient, if available and affordable.

The clockwork radio

Vocabulary

1 a written version of something that was originally spoken, such as a speech or conversation

2 d) a place where radio or TV programmes are made. (Note the question asks for the meaning *here* – (c) is an acceptable definition of 'studio' but not as used here.)

3 d) one that someone else has owned

4 a) no

b) somewhere a long way from the main towns and cities of a country, somewhere difficult to reach

5 a) unable to read or write

b) literate

Ask if students know any other words which have a negative form with the prefix 'il-' – legible / illegible and legal / illegal are the two most common pairs.

6 a) without the power to do something because of illness or injury

b) unable to move because of illness or injury. Therefore people who are paralysed are disabled, but a disabled person may not be paralysed – he or she might have lost an arm or leg, or be deaf or blind.

Note that 'paralysed' is often use figuratively in expressions such as 'paralysed with fear'. Another example: The transport in the city was paralysed by the sudden fall of heavy snow.

7 engineer

Note that a mechanical engineer is an expert with engines; a civil engineer designs and builds roads, buildings and bridges.

Understanding

1 c) electricity

2 False – clockwork radios have mechanisms like all clocks used to have – a spring that is wound up with a key.

3 True (lines 8–11)

4 False – clockwork radios *are* portable, but so are small transistor radios that use batteries. Trevor Baylis's contribution was to invent the clockwork portable radio.

5 information about how to keep healthy (lines 34–35)

6 a) It does not need batteries and so is cheap to operate.

b) It needs to be wound up every forty minutes. (Students may also suggest that if a clockwork radio breaks it might be difficult to repair.)

7 False – we are not told this. We are told that the radios are made in South Africa. (line 45)

8 False – he has helped disabled people by inventing special tools and giving them work by making the radios. The person who slipped on a banana skin (lines 48–53) is given simply as an example. 'You' (line 48) is here used in the sense of 'anyone'.

9 They could be easily used by disabled people. (line 55)

10 False (lines 64–65)

11 False (lines 68–70)

Discussion

This article raises several other topics which you might find appropriate to discuss with students. They should relate them to their own lives and communities where appropriate.

Suggestions for topics are: (1) Disabled people and how they can be helped in and by the community (2) Illiteracy (3) Health – particularly in the community, and how it can be improved
(4) Inventions (get students to suggest some useful ideas; maybe they would like to be inventors)
(5) Future careers

UNIT 6

Daring rescues

The Rescue

Pre-reading discussion

rescue: saving from danger; setting free

The writing of notes as suggested is of course optional, but discussion, sharing ideas, and writing notes, together with the reading of the passages themselves provide stimulation and material for an eventual writing task. You may also be able to bring into class newspapers, local or overseas, with accounts of rescues. These need not be in English – the objective is to stimulate interest in the topic of rescues and generate lively oral and written work.

Vocabulary work

1 to rock is to move or cause to move from side to side or backwards and forwards.

Elicit another meaning – a large piece of stone.

2 A cushion is a bag filled with soft material to make a seat more comfortable. When used to support the head in bed, it is called a pillow.

3 your arms and legs

4 the sharp, hooked nails a cat has in its paws

5 a) a measure of length (a metre is 1.0936 yards)

Explain if necessary that in traditional British and US measures, there are twelve inches in a foot and three feet in a yard. Metric units for weights and measures are used widely in the United Kingdom, though many people there still use the traditional measure. The traditional measures are still used in the United States. Note that Hal Summers is an American writer.

b) a piece of enclosed land with a hard surface, for example behind a house or other building

6 a) stick

b) caught – unable to move

c) fastened (with glue / paste / adhesive)

7 'as it was getting dark'

8 a) moving about wildly

b) Because it is windy.

Point out that 'toss' may also mean to throw up in the air: John tossed the coin, and shouted 'Heads!' It came down tails, so Paul won and said his team would start the game. Note too: He tossed in his sleep.

9 A round object (such as the glass shade round a lamp). A model of the Earth is called a globe.

10 a) a person who is walking

b) a place marked across a road where pedestrians should be able to cross in safety, as traffic will stop for them

11 All right!

Be sure students understand that 'OK' expresses or asks for agreement. It is informal English, generally only used in speech: OK? / Is that OK? It may be spelt Okay, and with or without full stops.

12 a small, hand-held electric lamp containing its own battery

Students may remember 'torch' being used in the traditional sense – when reading about the Olympic Games (line 52, page 13).

13 b) told it had done wrong

14 father and mother

Organisation of the poem / Understanding

The poem divides after line 16 (after section 3)

Section 1

1 'The boy climbed up into the tree.' (line 1)

2 Because the boy was climbing high and the branches were thin and therefore not so strong there. / The wind was blowing.

Ask where this is mentioned in the poem: fluttering leaves (line 10), 'the wind blew so' (line 11), the wind rising (line 29).

3 The cat could not talk, but the boy imagined the cat was thinking these words.

4 that it is soft

Section 2

5 'So up he climbed' (line 8)

6 'he would have flown if he had let go'

7 fly

8 No, he would have fallen to the ground.

9 Hal Summers is suggesting that the wind is so strong the boy would not have fallen straight down to earth, but would have moved horizontally, flying. This is of course not true, but writers, and specially poets, often write imaginatively. He is stressing the power of the wind.

Section 3

10 The boy picked up the cat and turned around ready to climb down.

Section 4

11 'His heart-beats knocked as he tried to think' (line 20)

12 a) He felt very frightened.

b) He planned to put the cat in a 'lower chink' and then to get back to the ground with it.

Elicit that the chink was probably the space between two branches. Note we also use 'chink' (as verb and noun) to describe the sound of glasses, coins, etc. touching.

13 The cat stuck its claws into him (line 23). It was very frightened – 'with a cry of alarm' (line 22).

14 He had climbed up using two legs and two arms. He would have to climb down with only two legs and one arm (as he was holding the cat) and this would be much more difficult. (Be sure students understand that a limb may mean either an arm or a leg.)

Section 5

15 'So there he was stuck' (line 28)

16 Because it is firm and safe.

17 Note that line 26 can be interpreted in two ways. Either: he realises that the ground is hard – that he would hurt himself if he fell on it, or: he realises that it would be hard (difficult) to get down. (You may point out that though generally we should make our meaning absolutely clear, sometimes poets deliberately write with ambiguity, so that in fact we can understand *both* meanings.) He changes his mind very quickly – within a minute (lines 26–27).

18 he was so frightened

19 paralysed

Section 6

20 b) Hope!

21 a) 'What on earth are you doing up there? / up that tree? / with that cat?'

b) His son interrupted him with the words in line 32.

Section 7

22 the lights on the pedestrian crossing and the street lights

23 beautiful

Section 8

24 He was frightened and was ready to cry. However, he tried hard not to, and just as he was going to cry, his rescuers came.

25 Because he had to find a ladder – perhaps this was difficult, maybe he had to borrow one.

26 Because he was cold and / or frightened.

Section 9

27 b) How the cat was rescued

Explain how the other topics all support this idea and show how it was done.

28 to hold the ladder steady

29 The boy already had the cat. He gave it to his father. The father gave it to the mother. The mother gave it to the boy's brother.

Section 10

30 'The parents … too' (line 53) or 'And all of them went indoors to supper'. (line 55)

31 He compares the moon to the cat.

32 The first part describes how the boy caught the cat. The second part describes how the boy then had to be rescued.

Ask which part students think is the more important, and why – the second part, because here the boy is in danger, and the poem describes his feelings.

33 He was high up. It was windy. It was dark. He had to carry the cat, so could not use both hands.

Spelling – silent consonants

section 4: o*h*, hi*gh*, wou*l*d, lim*b*s, *k*nocked, ei*gh*teen

section 8: num*b*, thou*gh*, wou*l*d

Note also: lea*r*n, ha*r*d, hea*r*t and a*r*m, in section 4, and finge*r*s, fi*r*st, bu*r*st in section 8. Most native speakers of English would not sound the 'r' here, though some, for example Scots people, would. See also in these sections: fou*r*, lowe*r* and he*r*, and fathe*r*, mothe*r*, ladde*r*, younge*r*, brothe*r*, where native speakers pronounce the final 'r' only if a vowel follows, eg four oranges. Furthermore, final 'g' is only pronounced before a vowel: so it is not pronounced in 'having come up' or 'feeling cold', but is pronounced in 'having a party'.

doubt	knife	write	scenery
knob	listen	wrong	island
lamb	wrist	foreign	answer
wrap	know	autumn	often
half	knuckle	sword	handsome
hour	chemistry	sign	palm
calm			

The Scarlet Pimpernel

Vocabulary work

1 A hood covers the top and back of the head. It looks rather like a bag, and is often fastened to a coat. A mask hides the face partly or completely. A hat describes any type or shape of head covering.

2 a round container, usually made of wood, with flat ends

Ask if students know what the barrel of a gun is – the long tube through which the bullet is fired.

3 b) loaded

4 a) 1 papers (line 14). (Point out that 'papers' often mean documents such as identity cards and passports.)
2 right (line 14)

b) 1 innocent (line 14) 2 empty (line 13)

5 as quickly as it can

6 shouted

7 a) You move your head up and down.

b) 'Yes' – that you agree with someone.

c) to shake your head

Remind students about using 'head' with 'shake' (Vocabulary work, point 9, page 37).

8 very frightened

9 a) took his sword out of its sheath

b) a sheath is the close-fitting case a knife or sword is kept in. (To sheathe means to put a knife or sword in its sheath; to unsheathe means to take it out. Note the final 'e' of verb.)

10 a) a stupid person

b) idiotic. (Point out spelling '-ic' which a number of adjectives use, eg fantastic.)

11 Example: A big reward was offered for the return of the stolen jewels.

12 the loud noise heard after a flash of lightning; the noise of the horse's hooves on the road was like thunder

Point out how 'thunder' can be used to describe how someone speaks / shouts, particularly when angry: 'Don't do that!' my father thundered. Also: We heard the thunder of guns in the distance.

13 As used here: a device for removing a person's head with a heavy falling blade. (It was invented by a Frenchman, Dr Guillotine, at the time of the French Revolution. The word also describes a small machine with a long blade used to cut paper or metal.)

Understanding

1 a) False – the book is called 'a novel' in line 1. The Scarlet Pimpernel was not a real person. However, the French Revolution, when the story is set, was an historical event.

b) False – note 'as well' (line 3). Both guilty and innocent suffered.

c) False – the driver was an innocent farmer. (line 28)

d) False – the 'captain' was the Scarlet Pimpernel himself in disguise. (line 29)

e) True (line 26)

2 France

3 to prevent the escape of such people as the Scarlet Pimpernel was helping

4 Because they looked harmless (innocent) and they had the correct papers. (lines 13–14)

5 thirteen altogether – the captain and twelve (a dozen) other horsemen (line 16)

6 a) He was pretending to be chasing the cart, so he had to be seen moving as quickly as possible.

b) Perhaps to impress the guard – the guard would feel he was an important man that he would have to obey instantly and without question.

7 Possible reasons: Because of his splendid uniform. / He did not have time to think, everything happened so quickly. / As a soldier he was used to obeying army officers without question.

8 the Scarlet Pimpernel and his 'soldiers'

9 The 'captain' was so angry, the guard must have felt sure he had done the wrong thing in letting the cart through the gate.

10 a) less than half an hour ago

11 We use 'explode' when talking about a bomb. The captain became angry as quickly and as dangerously as a bomb explodes. (Note we also commonly say someone 'explodes' with laughter.)

Punctuation

The people on horseback were not really a captain and his soldiers, and the quotation marks are used to draw attention to this. A signature is written – the picture of a flower is not what we would usually consider to be a signature, so 'signed' is being used in an unusual way.

Ask if students remember 'signed' being used in a similar way, and marked off in quotation marks in an earlier unit – see page 7, line 5.

Dolphins

Man's best friend?

Pre-reading discussion

Elicit that dolphins are large creatures that live in the sea. (That dolphins are not fish, but mammals is explained in lines 8–11. You do not need to state this now, though some students may know and volunteer the information.) You might develop a discussion on swimming – who can / can't, where students swim, etc. You may ask students whether they think some, but not other animals should be kept in zoos, and what justification there is for it.

Vocabulary work

Paragraph 1

1 a) joy (line 7) b) leaping (line 6)
c) slim (line 3) d) frequently (line 4)

2 a) smooth
b) They are made as smooth as possible so that air moves easily over them, and so they can go more quickly and use less fuel.

Paragraph 2

3 a) a sound sent back, such as that of your voice within a valley, or in a large room
b) Dolphins, whales and bats send out sounds, some of them too high for humans to hear, which bounce back and are heard by the animal. Their brain is able to use the echo to tell them where objects are around them, though they cannot see them, due to size, poor light or poor sight.

4 a) feed (a baby or a young animal) on milk from the breast
b) animal or bird that is hunted by another one for food

Paragraph 3

5 a similar type of animal or plant. Example: The lion and the tiger are different species of cat.

6 about (line 17)

7 A turtle is an animal (reptile) that has a shell on its back and spends much of its time immersed in water; a seal is a mammal that lives mainly in the sea but comes to the land to breed.

Note both these items, and particularly the second, are best explained by giving the equivalent in the students' first language, unless their dictionaries contain illustrations.

Paragraph 4

8 a) greatest (line 26) b) sadly (line 27)

9 accidentally (line 31)

10 each year / every year

11 Examples: The thief threatened the shopkeeper with a gun. / Fishing nets are a threat to dolphins.

Paragraph 5

12 They mix with them. / They swim with / alongside them.

13 'soothed' (line 38)

14 The shore is where sea and land meet.

15 gently pushing. (Point out that 'nudge' can be used as a verb or a noun – a nudge is a gentle push.)

Paragraph 6

16 a) allow (line 54) b) entertain (line 51)

17 a large ring of wood or metal

18 a place where dolphins are kept

19 captivity (line 48)

Spelling

1 The verb may be altered by doubling a final consonant, or by dropping a final 'e'.

2 paragraph 1: interesting, circling (altered: circle), swimming (altered: swim), leaping

paragraph 5: suffering, swimming (altered: swim), helping, protecting, drowning, nudging (altered: nudge)

Understanding

You could warn the students to read the questions very carefully.

1 a) False – dolphins are certainly interesting, but they are mammals, not fish. (lines 10–11)

b) False – 'also' (line 22) means that turtles, etc. are eaten *in addition to* the fish and squid that all other types of dolphin eat.

c) False – 'Dolphins never attack humans' (line 32). Killer whales are not mentioned as an exception. Do not be misled by their name!

d) False – they are hunted in 'only a few areas'. (line 29)

e) True (lines 36–40)

f) True (lines 10–14)

2 a) The senses are sight, hearing, smell, taste and touch.

b) smell

c) they live underwater so don't need to be able to smell

3 Perhaps the dolphins are simply curious / inquisitive and wanting to know more about the people in the water, wondering what they are. Maybe they might equally push them out to sea!

4 'As if' (line 7) suggests that we may see the jumps as showing joy, but perhaps they leap for other reasons.

5 to test the dolphins' skill at echo-location – finding or avoiding objects by sending out sounds and receiving echoes

6 The writer certainly does not state any objections to keeping dolphins in captivity. The word 'happily' in line 48 strongly suggests he approves of doing this. He also stresses that keeping dolphins like this is useful for scientific studies, not just for entertainment. Students may not agree with him, but here they are asked to state the writer's view. They can put forward their views when the class looks at Discussion, point 2, page 62.

7 They need to fill their lungs with air, because they are mammals, not fish.

8 Their beautiful bodies, the way they leap into the air, the way they can communicate by making sounds, the way they seem to want to be with humans, and their intelligence (eg in learning tricks) are all attractive. They are in many ways like humans.

9 Because, unlike other dolphins, they attack other creatures.

10 Perhaps because dolphins are so friendly and in so many ways like ourselves.

Ask the students if they know that many ancient Greeks believed that to kill a dolphin was as bad as to kill a human being, and that it should be punished as murder.

11 a) a fish which must hunt dolphins for its food

b) Man – who does not need to hunt dolphins, but sometimes does so deliberately, or accidentally kills them in his fishing nets.

Paragraphing

1 a) He finds them interesting and attractive.

b) Dolphins are slim and streamlined; they often circle boats; they may swim close to shore; they leap into the air.

2 a) Dolphins are warm-blooded; they suckle their young; they breathe through lungs; and they communicate through sounds.

b) They can use sound for echo-location.

3 size, speed, food, length of life
4 threats to dolphins / their enemies
5 relationships between humans and dolphins in the wild / in the sea
6 Dolphins in captivity

Pronouns

a) dolphins b) the dolphins'
c) the keepers' / the killer whales'

Discussion

2 Points against keeping animals in captivity: unnatural; animals do not have enough room for exercise; and they might find the constant presence of human beings disturbing.

Points for: it gives most people an opportunity of seeing many types of animals; it arouses their interest so they might then give support in helping to look after animals in the wild who are threatened with extinction; it gives opportunity for close scientific observation and experiments; some species have been saved by breeding in zoos, and then returning offspring to the wild.

Spelling

Note: words in the list in italic have been altered:

hitting	*hopping*	
hoping	*beginning*	creeping
preferring	benefiting	frying
seeing	sawing	
staying	*slipping*	journeying
profiting	sailing	sleeping

Arion and the dolphin

Note the pronunciation of Arion, which has three syllables, with the stress on the second syllable: A - ri – on.

Vocabulary work

Sections 1,2 and 3

1 a) farewell (line 23). (Explain this is an old English word, not generally used in modern English. The writer probably used it as he was writing about an old Greek legend.)
b) invited (line 3)
c) return (line 11)
d) awarded (line 17)
e) wandered (line 1)
f) received (line 5)
g) ships (line 11)
h) harbour (line 21)

2 a piece of land surrounded by sea

3 Examples:
a) I have just received an invitation to Jane's birthday party.
b) Ruth promised to send me a letter every week, but she never writes.
c) What would you most miss about your country if you lived abroad?
d) I tried to persuade Mike to come to the cinema, but he said the film was boring.
e) Barbara refused to sing because she had a sore throat.

Section 4

4 around
5 a) plotted (line 27) b) cabin (line 25)
6 a) poor b) safe
7 a) entire (line 28)
b) hurt (line 29)
c) reach (line 33)
d) allow (37)
e) leap (line 39)
f) finest (line 40)
8 live
9 a) Examples: Jenny made up her mind to improve in maths, worked hard, and

came top in the examination. / My father wants a new car, but cannot make up his mind which model to buy.

b) decide

10 a) a musical sound

b) A short letter or a few words you write down to remind yourself of something. You might make notes of something you had read in a book.

Sections 5–9

11 a) love. ('Like' is possible, but 'love' is stronger and probably better here.)

b) very pleased. ('Delighted' is stronger than 'pleased', so better to add 'very'. 'Overjoyed' could also be used.)

c) extremely surprised / shocked

d) a few

Note: an opportunity to remind students of the difference between 'few' (not many) and 'a few' (several). Compare: My cousin has few friends, though she has been at the school for a year now. / My cousin has already made a few friends at her school.

12 a) a long time

b) extremely frightened

c) fear

13 Example: (1) My brother pretended not to care that he was not picked for the team, but I knew he was very disappointed. (2) The thief was punished by three years in prison.

14 Dying by sinking under water and not being able to breathe.

Understanding

1 a) False – whenever he stopped to sing, people also stopped to listen to him – but they did not ask him to sing. (lines 1–2)

b) False – the King of Corinth invited him to live with him in the Royal Palace. We are not told exactly who invited Arion to Sicily, but it was probably the king who gave him the first prize. (line 17)

c) False – 'The gold does not interest me' (line 9)

d) True (line 17)

e) False – the dolphins were attracted by his song (line 43). The story does not say he knew they were there or that they would come.

f) True – 'dolphins are very fond of music' (line 44)

g) True (lines 44–45)

h) False – delighted (line 48)

2 Greece (line 63), and we are told this is a Greek legend in the introduction – Corinth is in Greece.

3 Because the King liked Arion's singing so much.

4 that he return

5 They wanted his gold and treasure. (line 26)

6 a) He offered them the gold and other treasures he had won. (line 31)

b) The crew let Arion sing and this attracted the dolphin which saved him.

7 By returning to Corinth as he had promised.

8 They thought he was dead, and that they were seeing a ghost.

Story organisation

section 1: f
section 2: d
section 3: c
section 4: e
section 5: b
section 6: g
section 7: h
section 8: a
section 9: i

You could ask students write down the headings in the correct order. Then, without looking at the story, use them as prompts to recount the story. Students could work in groups of 5: Student A recounts sections 1 and 2; B section 3; C section 4; D sections 5 and 6; and E sections 7, 8, and 9.

Writing

You may decide to let students choose freely between options (1) and (2), or direct individuals to do one option. Option (1) is the easier option. If option (2) is made available, you might like to suggest where the exclamations and questions might go, and invite / suggest others.

If suitable, students could work in pairs. One would be Arion telling the story. The other would be the King providing exclamations and questions.

Good vibrations

This is a difficult passage. It will challenge even the better students. However, by using a dictionary and some information from the unit, students should be able to work out the meaning. You might like students to work in pairs or small groups. Here are definitions of key words:

mentally (line 1) – in the mind

handicapped (line 1) – unable to do something properly because of an illness or physical injury

session (line 3) – a period of time

neuro-stimulating (line 3) 'neuro' means to do with the brain; stimulating means to arouse, make to work better, so together – making the brain more active

therapy (line 4) – treatment

high-frequency noises (line 5) – very high sounds

motor neuron disability (line 6) is one that stops certain neurons (part of the brain) working properly so that a person cannot move around

autism (line 6) – a sort of mental disability

experts (line 7) – people who know a lot about a subject

co-ordination (lines 9–10) – the ability to move different parts of the body together in the right way

As easy as A B C

Turning pictures into words

Pre-reading discussion

1 It is true that these modern media are important and powerful, but in a modern society everyone needs to *read* for a wide variety of purposes. Ask students to suggest some. Obvious responses: for all types of learning at school and college, newspapers and magazines for current events, etc., posters / notices, labels on items such as food and medicines, instruction leaflets, non-fiction books. Fiction can be a great source of pleasure. Note that the passage 'Does reading really matter?', Student's Book 1, page 47 contains very useful ideas on this topic. We all need to *write* to keep notes and records and to write personal and business letters.

2 Elicit that signs are particularly useful in public places, where one symbol can instantly represent a whole phrase, eg Access for the disabled is available; when they have to be understood by people who speak different languages, eg at airports and at international sporting events, such as the Olympic Games; when people need information immediately, and at a distance, eg on roads.

3 Elicit that it might be easy to draw some objects, but it would take a lot of time, and not everyone is a good at drawing. Some objects would be too complicated to draw (eg an aeroplane would be easier than an airport). Abstract ideas (such as honesty), verbs, conjunctions, prepositions, and many adjectives, such as colours, would be hard. Note that the article suggests how picture writing could be modified to solve some of these problems. Do not provide this information now, it is enough to outline the problems.

Vocabulary work

Paragraph 1

1 but / however

Paragraph 2

2 c) unhappiness

3 a) took (line 15) b) in fact (line 18)
c) for (line 18)

Paragraph 3

4 system (line 24)

Paragraph 4

5 a) maybe b) very

Paragraph 6

6 whole (line 41)

Understanding

1 a) True – 'half a million' (line 1)
b) True – 'They first wrote by using pictures.' (line 3)
c) False – pictures can represent ideas. (line 5)
d) False – 'an eye with tears might mean sorrow' (lines 6–7)
e) a) True – 'a beautiful system of writing' (line 21)
b) False – this writing represented 'things, ideas and some sounds'. (lines 23–24)
f) False – the writer says *many* (not *all*) inventions are very simple. (line 31)
g) True – 'Any symbol can be used for an alphabet.' (lines 32–33)
h) False – each 'character' represents a whole *word* (line 42). The characters do not represent sounds as do the letters of an alphabet.
i) True – because each Chinese character represents a whole word or idea, not the sound of the word, as with a word written using an alphabet. (lines 43–44)

2 speaking (lines 1–2)

3 a) Motorcycles and cars are not allowed to enter. (The ring is coloured red and this denotes a warning or prohibition.)
  b) access for disabled people (by a ramp or sloping floor, rather than stairs), or toilets designed for wheelchair access
  c) Please put your litter / rubbish here.
  d) No smoking!

Ask what signs might be used to suggest: (1) no photography allowed – like the No smoking sign, but with a camera (and flash) instead of a cigarette; (2) (for motorists) you are approaching a school – two small children walking; (3) a restaurant – knife, fork, plate; (4) tea / coffee bar – tea cup; (5) a filling station – petrol pump; (6) a garage for repairs – spanner; (7) a hairdresser – comb and scissors. Invite students to describe other signs they have seen, or ask if they can make any up.

4 a) drawing
  b) photograph. (Explain that 'photo' comes from a Greek word meaning 'light'.)
  c) a drawing in the form of a line which sloped upwards as accidents increased from one year to another.

5 a) a large group of soldiers (more than just five) or even an army
  b) happiness

Ask students to suggest how the following might be indicated as ideographs. Suggested answers are Egyptian hieroglyphs, but other ideas are possible: (1) walking – two legs (2) wind – a sail (3) old age – one or two old people walking, maybe with sticks (4) eating – someone eating / a mouth (5) unhappiness – an eye with tears (6) to fly – a bird. Invite other ideas for ideographs – it could be done for homework and ideas shared later.

6 They are ideographs (because they represent the idea of a certain number – thus the idea of '5' is not represented by five lines (as it was in early ways of recording numbers).

7 a) horse – an ideograph because the chief was not on a horse, but in a canoe: the horse gives the idea of travelling
  b) eagle – an ideograph because there was no eagle present – the eagle gives the idea of bravery
  c) canoes – a pictograph because there were really canoes
  d) a man on horseback – a pictograph because there really was a chief

8 e) all of them (lines 23–24)

9 act

10 by writing

Paragraphs

1 The development of writing. Note the question asks not for the topic of this paragraph, but rather of the whole article, which is clearly about writing, not talking.

2 the first sentence of each paragraph

Pronouns

a) our ancestors (line 2)
b) the alphabet (line 30)
c) characters (line 38)

Road sign: motorists watch out for koala bears on the road

Spelling

neither	weigh	thief	fierce
deceive	niece	pierce	field
achieve	brief	receipt	eight
veil	height	friend	lieutenant
patient	conscience	view	

Ask if students know the two meanings of 'patient': (1) (adjective) keeping calm when annoyed or unable to do something; (2) (noun) a person receiving medical attention or care.

A new way of writing

Vocabulary work

Paragraph 1

1 a) blunt

2 a) bread or cake

b) in an oven

Paragraph 2

3 able to be easily read

4 particularly (line 16)

Paragraph 3

5 b) changed completely

6 a) glass

b) the window in front of the driver

7 a) like

b) enjoyable

8 a) 1 immediately

b) 3 keep

Prefixes to make words of opposite meaning

1 a) uncommon b) slowly

c) unimportant d) quiet

e) easy / simple f) unhappy

g) uninterestingly h) incorrectly

2 a) dissimilar b) illegibly c) disappear

Understanding

1 a) True (lines 1–3)

b) False – they used papyrus (line 7). *Then* paper was invented (line 8).

c) True – 'made from wood' (line 8)

d) False – it was invented in the middle of the nineteenth century. (lines 12–13)

e) False – the passage does not say this. It says typewriters were particularly important in business (line 16).

f) False – it was troublesome with a typewriter. (lines 18–19)

g) True (line 14)

h) True (lines 27–28)

i) True – writing is quicker. (line 37)

j) False – the passage says in '*most* English schools'. (line 39)

k) False – the passage says that *some* teachers believe this. (line 41)

2 Because a typewriter prints numbers and letters of the alphabet which are always clear and exactly the same however fast you type; in handwriting each letter is shaped individually.

3 You can change what you have written easily before printing it. You can store writing on a floppy disk or in the machine (on the hard disk). You can alter the size of letters very easily. You can check and correct spelling very easily.

These are mentioned in the text; students familiar with word processing may be able to suggest other advantages.

4 No – you need a computer for word processing. This equipment is expensive and even small ones are not easy to carry around. They need a mains electricity supply or batteries, which do not last long before they need recharging. On the other hand, pen and paper are cheap and portable. Moreover, writing by hand is more personal, better suited to personal letters, for example.

Ask students whether they would prefer a hand-written letter from a friend, even though perhaps badly written and not easy to read, to a typewritten / word processed one.

5 Because they are legible – easy to read.

Discussion

1 a) A fountain is an ornamental jet of water placed in gardens, town squares and parks.

b) a pen which has a container which you fill with ink

c) Fountain pens are more difficult to make and need special metal nibs, preferably of gold. Therefore they are much more expensive. They have to be filled with ink. The ink sometimes leaks from the pen.

Staying alive

Girl against the jungle

The passages in this unit come from one article, divided into short sections to make it easier to study. Students should enjoy the challenge of reading a true story which, though shortened, is printed just as it appeared in a magazine. The unit contains material for several lessons and maybe homework, too. The teacher may decide *either* to read and study each extract in turn *or* read the complete passage, leaving the questions until later. This second method is preferable, as it gives students a good overall grasp of the article, even if they do not understand everything, and does not diminish the excitement and suspense of the narrative.

Pre-reading discussion

a) lack of water and food, the effects of possible injuries suffered in the crash, lack of shelter (from rain, heat or cold) and maybe danger from wild animals

b) If the plane crashed in dense forest, the trees may hide the crash from other planes – so it might be better to walk. If it crashed in a desert, it is best to stay with the plane, as there is a good chance other aircraft will find it, and it would also provide shade in the daytime. It is impossible to survive long in open desert.

c) Desert offers the best chance of rescue if you have enough food, water and shade. On the other hand, forests might provide water and food (roots and berries).

d) The plane would have sunk, leaving little or no traces for rescuers to see. Flotation equipment is limited. However, in the daytime rescue planes could spot you, unless a storm blows up. A passing ship may see you. Food and drink are a problem, and exposure, too, if rescue is not swift.

Introduction

Vocabulary work

1 jungle (line 3) (Explain it describes only tropical forests.)

2 a) vanished (line 1)
  b) courage (line 4)
  c) recounted (line 5)
  d) emerged (line 3)

3 a) covered a large area

4 only

5 d) refusing to give up

Understanding

1 a country in South America

You could ask students to do some research on the country.

2 Because there is a vast amount of sparsely populated land consisting of huge, thick forests and high mountains, it could be difficult for rescuers to see survivors from the air, and if they did, aircraft and helicopters would have problems in finding places to land. There are no roads through the thick jungle, so it would be impossible for rescuers to reach the crash quickly overland. The survivors would lack food, water and medical supplies. There might be danger from wild animals.

The material for this question has been largely covered in the pre-reading discussion, so this is an opportunity for revision and for students who were previously less forthcoming to offer responses.

Part 1

Vocabulary work

1 b) happy

2 b) not often
3 c) tops
4 the line between sky and the land

Understanding

1 She was going with her mother to spend Christmas with her father. Also, she enjoyed flying.
2 Such delays were common in Peru.
3 The take-off was smooth and trouble-free, there was the usual meal, the stewardesses were smiling and some passengers went to sleep.
4 a) a great ocean, to the west of North and South America stretching to Japan, China and Australia
b) a great mountain range running north to south in the west of South America
5 a flat piece of wood or plastic for carrying things on, such as crockery (plates, cups, saucers, etc.) and food

Finding a good title

Examples: A happy start to the holidays / We take off

You may need to guide students to good titles. In each section several things happen. Stress that a title should convey the *main* idea / theme / event of the section.

Part 2

Vocabulary work

1 pattering
2 a) up and down
b) horizontally
c) moves from side to side
3 that they came out very quickly
4 very great
5 a) lost consciousness (line 29)
b) jolt (line 22)

Understanding

1 She had flown in a bad storm in the United States. (lines 18–19)
2 a) probably struck by lightning (line 15)
b) She was fastened to her seat by her seat belt (line 26). She probably hit tree branches, which broke her fall. (line 28)
3 Perhaps the plane was struck by lightning and broke up in the air.

Finding a good title

Examples: Crash! / The crash! / We crash! / Disaster! / Disaster strikes!

Part 3

Vocabulary work

1 a) completely

Note also 'sound asleep'. Point out that this is a less common use of 'fast'. We also say 'to hold fast (tightly) to something', eg a rope.

b) quick
2 flat
3 trace (lines 34 and 36)
4 very / extremely surprised
5 strangely

Point out that 'odd' means unusual / strange. Elicit other means of 'odd' – the opposite of even, eg an odd number; or not matching: My brother often wears odd socks.

6 a) shocked (dizzy)

Understanding

1 She did not feel any pain.
2 She was not strong enough. She was dazed and not able to think clearly. (lines 45–46)

Finding a good title

Examples: The awakening / A cruel awakening / I awake in the forest

Part 4

Vocabulary work

1 c) cruel
2 c) travelled
3 c) all the time
4 anywhere where people were living
5 met
6 cut off

Understanding

1 He / She lacks food. He / She dies of hunger.
2 b) although her back was hurting
3 They laid eggs under the skin which turned into larvae. These caused dangerous sores on her skin.
4 a) She found a stream and thought that if she followed the current she would eventually reach a river.
  b) She thought there would be people living near the river, or maybe sailing on it.
5 a) no
  b) It was a bad thing, because it meant they had not encountered men / hunters. Therefore Juliane was not likely to find people who could help her.

Finding a good title

Examples: Walking through the jungle / I start to walk / A terrible walk / I search for the river

Part 5

Vocabulary work

1 a) trouble
  b) break

Elicit / explain that 'to snap' suggests to break sharply, especially with a noise; also to shut with a sharp noise: She snapped the lid of the box shut; also to seize with teeth: The dog snapped at my leg.

  c) great pain. (Point out that 'agony' is a stronger word than 'pain'.)
2 the pointed end
3 twelve

Understanding

1 She would have to have her arm amputated.
2 So she could dig out the larvae.
3 Towards the sea – the strong current swept her off her feet. (line 88)

Finding a good title

Examples: Rescued! / Saved! / Safe at last! / I reach the river

What can you remember?

There are 30 questions. This exercise is suited to either individual or group work, depending on the ability of the class, etc. For example:

- **if students work individually, they can answer just one question each, or a number of questions, or every question;**
- **if students work in groups, give them each a set of questions. Each group writes out its' answers after consulting together, and then shares its' answers with the rest of the class.**

1 a) She was called Juliane Koepcke.
  b) She was 17 years old.
  c) She was flying from Lima in Peru.
  d) She was with her mother.
  e) They were going to see her father.
  f) The passengers felt relaxed.
  g) Yes – everything seemed normal.
2 a) A storm started: there was rain and lightning.
  b) The plane moved up and down and rocked from side to side.

c) The passengers screamed.
d) Her mother thought they were going to die.
e) Juliane saw flames coming from the wing.
f) She felt herself flying through the air, still strapped to her seat.
g) In the air above the forest.

3 a) She was awoken by the rain.
b) There were no other survivors.
c) She felt no pain.
d) She had a broken collarbone, a swollen eye, a bump on her head, and a small wound on her foot.

4 a) She started to walk.
b) She hoped to find a big river.
c) She had only a few sweets.
d) The sun burnt her back.
e) She was bitten by horseflies and mosquitoes.
f) The bites were dangerous because the insects laid eggs under her skin, and these hatched out into larvae.
g) She feared her arm might have to be amputated.
h) The animals she met were not afraid of her.
i) This meant they were not used to human beings, so there were probably no people nearby who could help her.

5 a) She made a ring into a knife to remove the larvae.
b) When she reached the river, she began to swim downstream, taken by the strong current.
c) She met three men who helped her.

Pronouns

1 the plane (line 5)
2 planes not leaving on time in Peru (line 6)
3 the plane (line 20)
4 that the dress was not torn (lines 41–42)
5 my back (line 50)
6 eggs (line 63)
7 larvae (line 64)
8 animals (line 67)
9 arms (line 69)
10 doctors or surgeons
11 the ring (line 82)

Spelling

The corrected words appear in *italic*.

carefree	*boarded*
jungle	*welcome*
worried	*rarely*
passengers	*stewardesses*
collected	breakfast
pattering	vertically
screams	*shaking*
moment	cauliflower
consciousness	*empty*
tremendous	*sloping*
glasses	*collar*
dazed	*mosquitoes*
impossible	*tweezers*
horrible	*swollen*
spiral	*centimetre*
barefooted	

Writing

Students are asked to use the format of a newspaper report. In newspaper reports, headlines and the first introductory sentence are very important. Invite students to suggest these.

Examples of headlines: Teenager's miraculous escape / 17-year-old girl survives jungle ordeal / Sole survivor!

The introductory sentence should sum up the story and engage readers' interest, for example:

A 17-year-old American girl has just had a miraculous escape. / A weary teenager has just walked out of the Peruvian jungle alive. She is the

sole survivor of an aircrash which killed over 80 passengers, including her mother.

Ask which opening students prefer, and why. The second is more gripping: we can 'see' two very dramatic situations – the crash and Juliane coming out of the jungle. It also gives more information, notably the number of dead, and the fact about Juliane's mother.

You could use the following model version as a dictation. The numbers of the answers covered by each sentence on page 82 (Student's Book) is given in brackets. Point out how *connecting words and phrases* have been used to link sentences. Sentences can of course be combined in other ways. Discuss these, but discourage students from overusing 'and'. Remind them that items combined by using 'and' should be related in some way, for example:

My name is Susan, and it is raining today. (wrong)

My name is Susan, and I hate being called 'Sue'. (correct)

It is raining today, and it has been raining for three days now. (correct)

Juliane Koepcke was flying with her mother in Peru from Lima to visit her father. (1a–e) They were very happy as the plane took off. (1f) Everything seemed normal, *but* soon a storm started, with rain and lightning. (1g–2a) The plane moved up and down and rocked from side to side, the passengers screamed, and her mother thought they were all going to die. (2b–d) *Then* Juliane saw flames coming from the right wing. (2e) *Next*, she felt herself flying through the air, and lost consciousness. (2f–g) She was *later* awakened on the ground by the rain. (3a) She saw no other survivors. (3b) Juliane felt no pain, though she knew she had a broken collarbone, a swollen eye, a bump on the head, and a small wound on her foot. (3c–d) *Hoping* to find a big river, she started to walk, *with* only sweets to eat. (4a–c) The fierce sun burnt her back, *and* she was bitten by horseflies and mosquitoes. (4d–e) *These* bites were dangerous *because* the insects laid eggs under her skin *which* hatched out into larvae, *and* Juliane feared that her arm might have to be amputated. (4f–g) *Unfortunately*, the animals she met were not afraid of her. (4h) *This* meant that they were not used to human beings, *so* there were probably no people nearby *who* could help her. (4i) She *then* decided to remove the larvae by making a ring into a knife. (5a) *At last*, she reached a big river and began to swim downstream. (5b) *Eventually*, she met three men *who* helped her to safety. (5c)

Emergency instructions

1 A leaflet is a small piece of printed material. It might consist of several pages, or be just one sheet.

2 'Exit' means a way out of eg a building. 'Emergency' means a sudden and unexpected danger. So an emergency exit is a door used only if, for example, the cinema caught fire.

3 You put air into it.

4 'chute' (line 6)

Explain that 'chute' rhymes with 'shoot' and that very few words in English which begin with 'ch-' are pronounced 'sh-'. Ask if students know a word which ends in '-chute'? – parachute.

2 1) Put out cigarettes, remove spectacles and shoes, and take out any false teeth.

2) Fasten your safety belt.

3) Put your seat into the upright position, then lean forward and rest your head on your arms.

4) When the plane has landed, unfasten your safety belt.

5) Put on your life jacket.

6) Jump on the chute and slide into the inflatable boat. (Ask why passengers should *jump* on the chute – this is the quickest and safest way of getting onto it.)

English Reading and Comprehension

Teacher's Book 3

Contents

UNIT 1

The fun they had

Pre-reading discussion

2 Elicit that schools give children the opportunity to talk to teachers about things they do not understand, and teachers can adapt their material to the needs of their classes. However, be sure students also understand the *social* advantages of schools: that children learn to get along with adults and other people, ie they come to understand how to live in a community and some of the responsibilities of citizenship.

Part 1

Vocabulary work

1 a daily written record of events and personal feelings, or of appointments for the future

2 The date was written at the top of the page.

Elicit the opposite of 'head of a page' – the foot.

3 smooth

4 b) strange

5 b) showing disrespect

6 a) adverb

b) sorrow

c) 2 unhappily

Understanding

1 twenty-second

2 Tommy's finding a real book

Ask why writers sometimes put a pronoun first in this way – to arouse our interest.

3 False – his grandfather's grandfather (great-great-grandfather) had mentioned a time when there were 'real' books (ie those printed on paper). (lines 4–5)

4 a) Because it was very old

b) No – because it is new.

5 Yes – because they find it so funny (strange).

6 a television screen, like Tommy's (line 12)

7 d) to learn / study / be educated – also to acquire social skills as elicited in the Pre-reading discussion

8 a room in the space under a pitched (sloping) roof, often used to store things

9 a) 'mechanical' (line 25)

b) We expect a teacher to be a person, not a machine. Alternatively students may suggest 'teacher' (line 25), because we do not usually consider that a machine is the same thing as a teacher; or possibly 'school' (line 24), because here it has a different meaning from our own usage.

10 No – they live in different houses – 'my house'. (line 18)

Part 2

Vocabulary work

1 a) very quickly

2 a) a very light blow, with the open hand

b) a young child, or a pet animal, such as a cat

3 a) 8

b) Add up all the income for all the months, and divide the total by the number of months.

4 a) in fact

Understanding

1 a) On the dashboard of a car, and inside clocks and watches of the traditional sort (analogue – with faces and hands).

Check if 'digital watch / clock' is known – where the time is shown with figures, eg 12:30.

b) They show measurements, such as time and speed.

c) It is an instrument which uses the sun's rays to tell the time. The sun casts a shadow from an upright marker onto a plate or dial marked like a clock face.

2 a machine / computer

3 No – easier questions. The County Inspector says 'the geography sector was geared a little too quick', which suggests it was asking questions too quickly, thus confusing the child. He made it go more slowly, so the questions would be easier for her to answer.

4 The general way in which she was improving. She might have some difficulties, but on the whole she was doing well.

5 friendly (he smiles at Margie and pats her on the head), kind (he gives Margie an apple), helpful and capable (he knows how to adjust the machine), reassuring (he says Margie's progress is generally satisfactory)

Part 3

Vocabulary work

1 Example: Jack wanted to win the race so he was disappointed when he only came second.

2 a) one without writing on it

b) a face which had no expression on it, which showed no emotion

3 a) clever

b) well dressed

Here 'smart' is used as an adjective. It can also be used as a verb in the sense of to give a stinging pain: My hand still smarts where I burned it. Also figuratively: I smarted with anger at his insults.

4 argue

Note the use of 'with' / 'about' with 'argue' here: Margie was not prepared to argue about that.

5 b) adapted. ('Changed' and 'altered' have similar meanings but 'adapted' is best: it suggests keeping something basically the same, but making special alterations / changes to suit particular circumstances. A book is adapted for the cinema. A person who lives in another country must adapt to its climate and customs. In the story, the changes to the machine are to make it suitable for a particular person.)

6 c) nevertheless. (''Despite that' / 'In spite of that' would also be good replacements.)

7 a) did not seem to care

Understanding

1 a machine

2 a) 'very superior eyes' (line 49), 'loftily' (line 51)

b) He was older. Perhaps he thought boys were superior to girls.

3 Because Margie did not understand what schools and teachers used to be – special buildings and people.

Here Tommy screams with laughter. Ask when else someone might scream – if frightened or in pain (the more common use).

4 a) the children could have continued talking

Part 4

Vocabulary

1 a) neighbourhood (line 95)

b) proper (line 91)

2 'Please put / place yesterday's homework in the proper slot.' (Check that students understand 'slot'. Ask what a slot machine is – a machine that delivers tickets, or articles such as drinks or chocolate when you insert money in the slot.)

Understanding

1 a special room in her own house

2 a) young people living centuries before Margie and Tommy – the present generation

b) in the past, which as the story is set in the future means 'now' – the present.

Discussion

1 Elicit that to Margie the idea of learning with other children is so wonderful that it seems like pure enjoyment. But we know that however much we may want to learn, like our teachers and enjoy most lessons, school also involves hard work, and sometimes doing tasks we do not want to do. So her ideas are not entirely accurate.

2 Margie's ideas amuse us. On the other hand, the story suggests serious questions about what is the best way to teach children, whether it is best to work in groups or singly, how far a teacher, especially with a large class, can adapt material to each student's interests and abilities, and how useful computers may be in teaching. Thus the story is both humorous and serious.

3 **An optional alternative topic for pair /group discussion would be the advantages and disadvantages of the system described in the passages.**

- **Advantages: students can go at their own speed and not be bored at a slower pace forced on them by the rest of the class, or worried because they cannot understand what the rest of the class finds easy; they do not have to spend time getting to school and back.**
- **Disadvantages: a human teacher can explain difficulties more easily than a machine; students lack contact with other students who can stimulate and help them; learning might get boring, lacking variety; at school we learn 'social skills' – how to behave with people of our own age and older people.**

Spelling

1 a) little

b) yellow

c) funny

d) moving

e) supposed

f) million

g) attic

h) hated

i) mechanical

j) sorrowfully

2 stories

Ask if students know what 'storey' (plural 'storeys') means – a floor in a building.

UNIT 2

The roof of the world

Nepal explored

Vocabulary work

Paragraph 1

1 b) far away

Paragraph 2

2 floor

3 a) urban (line 9)

b) 'Rural' means to do with the countryside, 'urban' means to do with the town or city.

4 a) most

b) mostly

Paragraph 3

5 'Porters' are usually people who carry luggage at hotels or railway stations. Here it means people who carry equipment on expeditions. The heavy loads mentioned help to convey the meaning.

6 expeditions (line 13)

Paragraph 4

7 a) 2 the language used by the government. (Explain this would be in law courts and government documents.)

8 a) the language a person learns first in life, as a young child

Paragraph 5

9 a) a serious problem

b) minor

10 happening over a wide area

11 discourage

Elicit other words beginning with 'dis-' with this negative sense, eg dishonest, discontinue. They might consult their dictionaries.

12 a) not being able to read and write

b) literacy

Elicit other words beginning with 'il-' with a negative sense, eg illegal and illogical, also (less common) illegitimate / illicit.

13 reduced (line 23)

Ask how 'increased' can be changed into a word of opposite meaning by using a different prefix – decreased.

14 improve (line 21)

Paragraph 6

15 'Export' means to sell goods to another country, 'import' means to buy goods from another country.

You may ask what goods the students' own country exports and imports.

16 necessary / vital

Paragraph 7

17 a) yearly/every year

b) help

18 He or she has finished working usually because he/she has reached a certain age.

19 A salary is money earned by working. A pension is received after a person has retired.

You can explain that 'salary' is the word used for payment to professional people and paid monthly. A 'wage' is the term used for payment to a non-professional worker and is paid weekly. You may explain that money paid by an individual to a professional person for a service is a 'fee' – it is paid to a doctor, a hospital, a college, a school and a lawyer.

Understanding

1 India

2 No – most live either in mountain valleys or on the plain (lines 6–7), and more people are now moving to the plain (lines 23–24).

3 **You may ask for the names of capital cities of other countries too.**

4 Because over 50 languages and dialects are spoken. (line 17)

5 Because malaria is not now so common there. (lines 22–23)

6 It is easier to travel on the plain, and easier to farm.

7 Because transport is difficult – there are poor roads and few railways. (line 28)

8 Because of the mountain scenery and unusual way of life, so different from modern cities, and of course some may want to climb mountains.

9 Yes – it provides employment for some of their people. (lines 12–13)

10 Because it produces only agricultural items, and these are difficult to export, and it has to import many essential goods.

Paragraphing

1 a) paragraph 3
b) paragraph 2
c) paragraph 1
d) paragraph 7

2 paragraph 4: What languages are spoken in Nepal?
paragraph 5: How well are health and education needs met in Nepal?
paragraph 6: Which countries does Nepal trade with?

3 paragraph 4: The languages of Nepal
paragraph 5: Health and education in Nepal
paragraph 6: Trade in Nepal and with India

Spelling

1 a) separate

Note the different pronunciation: sep-ret (adjective) / sep-er-ayt (verb) – ask which part of speech 'separate' is here – verb.

b) people c) capital d) malaria
e) agricultural f) machinery
g) textiles h) salaries i) dollars
j) notably

2 a) countries b) valleys c) armies
d) Sherpas e) languages

3 a) rural b) enough c) mountaineering
d) official e) illiteracy f) government
g) widespread h) paraffin i) annually
j) received

The boy from Nepal

Pre-reading discussion

Be sure students understand the difference between immigration and emigration (and immigrate / emigrate). Most countries allow in people who have skills which are useful to the community. They will not be ready to admit people who are poor, without skills and who will not be able to work. Nor will they want people who are known to be criminals.

Vocabulary work

Paragraph 1

1 You make them leave your country.

2 Examples: Paul promised to be at the station promptly at 10 o'clock, but he was half an hour late and we missed the train. / Jane made a promise to her sister to visit her in Australia, and she is going next week.

Be sure students know these three verbs commonly used with 'promise': 'make' / 'keep' / 'break'. Ask if Paul kept or broke his promise – he broke it.

Paragraph 2

3 bring / get

Paragraph 3

4 Examples: A reward of $10,000 has been offered for the capture of the thief. / Trevor was rewarded for all his hard study by coming top in the examinations. (Elicit which is the noun / verb here.)

Paragraph 4

5 a) letters
b) immediately
c) found / learnt
d) began

Paragraph 5

6 poor
7 A shepherd looks after sheep.
8 gold, coal, iron ore, silver, salt, lead, tin
9 a place where people are served meals for which they pay

Paragraph 6

10 a) a teacher. (The word 'tutor' usually describes a person teaching one student or a small group of students.)
b) He was employed by Richard Morley solely to teach Jayaram, ie he was not employed by a school or college.
11 After Richard Morley died.

Teach also the noun 'will' – a written list of who you want your possessions to be given to when you die; and the noun 'inheritance' – what is received in a will.

Paragraph 7

12 b) request
13 a place where you live all the time
14 a) fresh (line 29)
b) true (line 26)
c) allowing (line 28)
d) change (line 27)

Paragraph 8

15 a) inhumane (line 36)
b) clearly (line 36)

Paragraph 10

16 'dis-' (disobey)

Understanding

1 It is not stated explicitly, but we can guess it was to climb mountains in the Himalayas.
2 Because he had a weak heart. (line 10)
3 Because Basu Khadka had saved his life. (line 7)
4 To find out why Basu Khadka had stopped writing to him (line 14). (*Not* because Basu Khadka had died: he may have suspected this, but he discovered it only after arriving in Nepal.)
5 Communications by road and rail are poor in Nepal and many different languages are spoken.
6 Jayaram would need to learn to speak and read English as soon as possible. He would learn more quickly by himself with a tutor.

You might have a discussion on whether learning in a class has any advantages – students can help one another sometimes – and whether some subjects are taught better in small groups – in foreign languages students can get more practice in speaking in a smaller group. This might also be an opportunity for students to discuss their own experiences in learning English – how they learn best, what they find most difficult.

7 He did not ask for a permanent residence visa straight away and he did not give Jayaram's correct age.
8 Because Jayaram was not costing the British government or people anything as Richard Morley was rich and was paying for everything.

9 Because after living in England for several years he was happier and more at home in England than in Nepal.

10 The Home Office believed that laws have to be obeyed.

Paragraphing

Part 1

a) A sad death – paragraph 4
b) Saved by a guide – paragraph 2
c) A promise is made – paragraph 3
d) Return to Britain – paragraph 6
e) The son is found – paragraph 5

Part 2

a) The problem referred to in paragraph 7 is that the Home Office will not allow Jayaram to stay in England.
b) Paragraphs 8, 9 and 10 all give points of view about the problem.
c) Each gives a different point of view: paragraph 8 gives Richard Morley's, paragraph 9 gives Jayaram's, paragraph 10 gives that of the Home Office.

Punctuation

1 Jayaram is not Richard Morley's natural son – he is his adopted son.

3 (,) = commas optional

Richard Morley has finally won his six-year battle to keep his 'son', Jayaram Khadka, in England. Yesterday(,) Home Secretary Jack Straw reversed the decision of his predecessor, Michael Howard, and allowed Nepalese orphan Jay Khadka to stay in this country. Richard Morley and Jay are planning a short holiday in France to celebrate. Jay's father saved Mr Morley's life after a climbing accident(,) and in return Richard Morley promised to bring Jay up after his father's death. Unfortunately(,) the young Nepalese had no residence permit(,) and his age was given wrongly on his passport when he came to England.

'Justice has finally been done,' said Richard Morley on hearing the news.

A smiling Jay added, 'We are overjoyed.'

Discussion

2 **Elicit the main points: tourism brings money to a country and gives people work (as guides, in hotels and in shops), but sometimes people become unhappy if they feel tourists are very rich and they are very poor, and at times large numbers of tourists make some areas too crowded for local people.**

I remember that!

The need to remember

Vocabulary work

1 a list of instructions on how to make a particular dish

2 invent (line 24)

3 a) heroes are men, heroines women – people greatly admired for their bravery

b) hero, heroine

4 It disappears slowly.

Be sure students understand that 'fade' is often used of colours which lose their brightness, perhaps because of exposure to the sun, or washing.

5 a) time

b) better

6 It wakes you up in the morning.

7 assume (line 36)

Understanding

1 We need a memory to understand who we are, and so that we can make use of lessons that we have learnt in the past.

2 a) memory for sounds, physical memory

b) memory for sounds, verbal and physical memory

c) memory for smells, emotional memory

d) physical and verbal memory

e) memory for touch, emotional memory

f) physical memory

g) emotional and verbal memory.

Note that there may be some difference of opinion and discussion here.

3 We learned to ride or drive in the past, perhaps a long time ago – we keep this skill in our long-term memory. But we need to be aware of what we see around us on the road, eg road signs and traffic lights, as well as other vehicles and what they are doing – we use our short-term memory here, even if only for a few moments.

4 Most memories start to fade quite quickly and are replaced by others. When we do remember something, we only remember the main events of what has happened and may invent the rest, maybe for emotional reasons.

5 So that new memories can be stored and so we do not get overburdened by unhappy memories, which would make us ill.

6 a psychiatrist. (See vocabulary note on page 24.)

7 our visual memory

Point out that there are few sure rules of English spelling and we rely on our visual memory to remember the shape of the words in order to spell them.

Paragraphing

1 the second sentence

2 paragraph 2: Visual memory

paragraph 3: Verbal memory

3 Memories for emotions, smell, taste, touch, sound and physical movements

4 long- and short-term memories

5 the first sentence

6 a) forgetting

b) Paragraph 7 is about the normal process of forgetting. Paragraph 8 is about amnesia.

7 the third sentence

Spelling

a) **The most 'modern' words are the ones most recently added to English dictionaries, such as the names of modern inventions, ie 'photos', 'stereos', 'videos' and 'radios'. 'Pianos', 'studios' and 'solos' are not quite so modern, but are more modern than the names of some vegetables, fruits, etc. Even though 'zero' originated from Arabic many hundreds of years ago, it can be spelt either way.**

b) photos, potatoes, mangoes, tomatoes, stereos, mosquitoes, pianos, videos, echoes, volcanoes, zeros/es, radios, solos, studios

Exam help for students

Note that questions (a) and (b) are repeated with supplementary ones in the Understanding section, question 2, page 27.

Use mnemonics

Note that the *connecting phrases* are in *italic*.

sentence 1: e) clearly states the topic.

sentence 2: d) *using mnemonics* relates to *mnemonics ... using* in the first sentence.

sentence 3: a) *He* refers to the mnemotist in (d). (line 40)

sentence 4: f) *But we* contrasts with *he* (the professional mnemotist).

sentence 5: c) *For example* introduces an example of a *simple mnemonic* mentioned in the fourth sentence.

sentence 6: b) *This* refers to the letters given to musical notes referred to in the fifth sentence.

sentence 7: g) *Another example* relates to the first example (EGBDF) given in the fifth and sixth sentences.

Vocabulary work

1 **This question well illustrates that many English words, including 'simple' ones (that is short and commonly used ones), have more than one meaning, and that they can be used as different parts of speech. Students should be encouraged to use dictionaries when they are confused by what they read, even though they believe they already 'know' what a word means.**

a) a noun

b) 'tip' as noun: (1) the end of something, often pointed, or at the top, eg fingertips, the tip of the tongue, the tip of an iceberg; (2) a place where rubbish is placed, especially a public place; (3) money given (eg to a waiter or taxi-driver) as a reward, in addition to any normal charge.

'tip' as verb: (1) to lean over: The ship tipped to one side; (2) to empty, pour out: I tipped the sour milk away. / I tipped the sugar into the bowl; (3) to give a tip, eg money, as in meaning (3) of tip as a noun. Note also the expression 'walk on tiptoe'.

2 a) unusual

3 a) necessary

b) usually

c) maybe

d) remember

4 simple

5 a) A 'professional' is a person who performs an activity for pay – a professional footballer plays football as his regular employment.

b) A 'profession' describes work for which higher education is needed – so we speak of the teaching, medical and legal professions. A 'professor' is the teacher of the highest grade in a university.

c) amateur – an amateur footballer does not get paid, and plays the sport for enjoyment in his spare time

6 a piece of land surrounded by water

Understanding

1 To calculate the circumference and area of a circle. If the radius is R, the circumference is 2 pi R , and the area is pi R^2.

2 a) The first two paragraphs are laid out like paragraphs usually are, but then we have six paragraphs each with a 'bullet'.

Check that students know what 'bullet' usually means – a piece of metal fired by a gun – the word is also used to describe the round marks (•) used in this type of layout. Elicit that bullets fired by guns used to be ball shaped.

b) Many verbs are in the 'imperative' or 'command' tense – the tense used to give orders, for example 'Understand', 'Revise' (rather than: You should understand, or The student should revise).

3 a) The short, bulleted paragraphs make the instructions easier to understand, and the use of the 'command' / 'imperative' verbs makes the style more direct, as though a teacher or adviser were speaking directly to us.

b) No – this layout and use of verbs is best used when giving instructions.

c) Instructions on how to make or use something – recipes are a good example. Leaflets are often included with radios, cameras, washing machines, etc., and these may use this type of layout.

d) Open question – though students will probably agree that the format makes it easier to see there are six points and easier to remember them.

Spelling

1 psychologist. (Note also 'psychology' and 'psychiatrist' in the vocabulary box.)

2 a) knee
b) answer
c) bomb
d) chemist
e) thumb
f) plumber
g) autumn
h) design
i) wrist
j) pneumonia
k) rustle
l) wrap
m) foreign
n) handsome
o) comb
p) knock
q) condemn
r) receipt
s) half
t) doubt

Note: these words have been chosen not simply because they contain silent letters, but because they are useful common words. Be sure students understand and can use them. Moreover, because they cover a range of topics, they can be used as points for vocabulary development – so 'knee', 'wrist' and 'thumb' for parts of the body; 'plumber' for various occupations; 'pneumonia' for illnesses and injuries, etc.

Some memory activities

4 Mum (for mother), Dad (for father) are the most common. Mummy and Daddy are more commonly used by younger children. Grandad / Grandpa for grandfather. (Note that the spelling 'granddad' is also used.)

The game tests short-term verbal memory.

A long time ago!

Vocabulary work

1 b) clearly

2 bright green

Note the common phrases: a vivid memory, a vivid story / account.

3 touching lightly, gently, with the open hand – not hitting. We pat people on the back to congratulate them. (See also Unit 1 Vocabulary work, point 2, page 9.)

4 a) frail (line 15)
  b) sure (line 27)
  c) exactly (line 27)

Understanding

a) false

b) Patting is a gentle and affectionate form of touching. Maybe Elizabeth had a younger baby sister or brother. The grandmother in bed, frail, and with a bedcap might have looked like a baby. Elizabeth was probably showing affection and sympathy.

Punctuation

A woman suffering from amnesia (1) could remember nothing of her family. Her children asked her to tell them a story about a horse. She had made up this story herself (2) and often told it them in the past. Now she could remember nothing about it. Then the children began to tell her the story. After a few minutes(,) (3) her face lit up. She stopped them, (4) and after a pause she continued the story. She could not remember all the details at once, (5) but with the help of her children she eventually remembered everything and regained her memory.

Note: all the full stops are *essential.* None of the above full stops can be replaced by a comma. Though it is always clear when a full stop, question mark or exclamation mark is needed, the use of a comma is often optional as this exercise illustrates.
Note:

(1) Here a comma must *not* be used. Some students may use one because in speaking we would make a slight pause. But a comma should not separate a subject (woman) from its verb (could remember).

(2) A comma *might* be used here, but if the subject (she) is not repeated after 'and', a comma is generally not used.

(3) A comma usually marks off an introductory adverbial phrase – but many writers would not use it for a *short* phrase, as here. So the comma is optional.

(4) The 'rule' outlined above for (2) suggests a comma *should* be used here as the subject 'she' is repeated.

(5) A comma is needed here – to separate long parts of a sentence, *particularly* before 'but'.

'her face lit up' means that she smiled / looked cheerful

Mission to the Moon

One giant leap

Pre-reading discussion

1 d) 1969

2 Americans

3 **Accept answers, but do not give information as answers are given in the passage.**

Vocabulary work

1 a) moved

b) Examples: Stir the paint before using it! (Transitive – with an object.) When the alarm clock sounded, Kevin stirred in his sleep, but did not wake up. (Intransitive – without an object.)

Point out that 'stir' can be used transitively or intransitively. Ask also whether 'stirred' is used transitively or intransitively in line 3 – transitive: 'eagle' is the subject and 'Moon dust' is the object of 'stirred'.

2 came down

3 a) to climb up to a window (to rescue someone) or down from a window (to escape)

b) to reach something high up, eg on a shelf, or to paint something high up, eg a window frame

c) a set of bars / steps / rungs held between two wooden or metal posts, or two ropes, and used for climbing up and down

4 a) a person who travels into space

b) astrology (astrologer / astrological), astronomy (astronomer / astronomical). Using a dictionary will explain the difference: astronomy is the scientific study of the stars and planets; astrology is not a science: an astrologer believes that by studying the stars he/she can say what will happen to people in the future.

You may add that 'astronomical' is now often used to mean 'very large': An astronomical amount of money is spent on advertising.

5 a) a seat hanging by ropes or chains which children sit on to swing backwards and forwards

b) a noun

6 A billion most commonly now means 1,000,000,000 (a thousand million). Formerly, and especially in British English, it meant 1,000,000,000,000 – a million million.

7 a) a very large man, especially one much taller than could be in real life, and one whom we hear about in some traditional stories.

b) very large: a giant box of chocolates, a giant oil company

8 jumping

9 put down

10 a jump on one foot – or with two feet together. (Explain that 'hop' is also a verb: birds and kangaroos hop.)

11 went around / circled

12 finished / completed

13 b) detached from the Command Module. (It has the sense of no longer being needed or used, being thrown away.)

14 A blaze (noun) means a fierce fire; if something blazes (verb) it burns strongly and brightly.

15 'Shield' originally meant a flat piece of strong material (usually metal) held by a fighter for protection – it is now used to describe anything that protects in a similar way. ('Shield' can also be used as a verb.)

Make sure students understand that as the module returns through the atmosphere, it gets very hot (because of air friction – the air rubs against the sides of the module) and a special metal shield protects it.

16 dived

You might give a clue: 'What do you do when you enter water head first?' and / or give 'v' as the middle letter.

17 travelled

18 cars, buses, vans, trucks, lorries. ('Lorry' is used in British, not American, English. Students may also suggest carts, drawn by animals.)

19 without people in them

20 maybe

Understanding

1 a) He was in the lunar module 'Eagle', which had just landed on the Moon.

b) Mission Control was on Earth.

2 The eagle is the national symbol of the United States.

3 a) on the Moon

b) It is an apt name because the Moon is so quiet – but of course it is not a sea, as there is no water on the Moon.

4 The men at Mission Control had been anxious for the safety of the spacecraft and its crew. They were so worried they could hardly breathe. When they knew everything was all right, they felt they could breathe again normally.

Mention 'to hold your breath' – when anxious about something: We held our breath as the helicopter lifted the survivors from the boat.

5 a) A step is the normal movement we make when walking; a leap is a jump.

b) Neil Armstrong meant that he had just walked in an ordinary way on the Moon, but that the achievement of reaching the Moon was a great advance, something shared by all mankind, from every race and country, because it showed what human beings can do.

6 The Moon dust had not moved for millions of years.

7 A large animal found in Australia. It travels fast by jumping and its young grow up in a pouch (bag) outside the mother's stomach.

8 Because the pull of gravity is so much less on the Moon – and the lunar module had only to rise a relatively short distance to rejoin the Command Module.

9 Because it was so hot.

10 The Command Module was descending by parachute, but it would still land heavily. The sea would act as a 'cushion'. Also, it could not damage anything in the sea – there would be no houses or people. Further, it would not have to land at an exact place – the recovery ship could easily sail to wherever the module landed.

Punctuation

Perhaps the question which is most asked about space is whether life exists elsewhere in the universe. We do not know. We know that there is no life on the Moon*. We know there is no life on any of the planets that circle the Sun*. However, we must remember that our sun is only one among billions of stars. Many of these stars are orbited by planets. On one of these, life may exist.

*** Note: 'moon' and 'sun' may be written with or without a capital letter.**

A comma is usually placed after 'however' at the beginning of a sentence. A comma is used in the last sentence after a long introductory adverbial expression. No comma would be used if the sentence were written: Life might exist on one of these planets.

Paragraphing

1 paragraph 1: first sentence
paragraph 2: third sentence
paragraph 3: first sentence
paragraph 4: first sentence
paragraph 5: fourth sentence
paragraph 6: second sentence
paragraph 7: first sentence

2 a) paragraph 5 b) paragraph 3
c) paragraph 1 d) paragraph 2
e) paragraph 4

3 The first sentence of paragraph 6 sums up all the previous five paragraphs.

Ask what the topic of paragraph 6 is – *further* visits to the Moon – this contrasts with the *first* visit.

4 The first sentence is the topic sentence.

Spelling

1 a) tranquillity b) ladder c) descended
d) astronaut e) difficult f) accomplished
g) atmosphere h) scientific
i) developments j) achievements

2 kangaroos

Note also 'zoo' / 'zoos'.

3 radioed

Note that the plural of radio (n) does not have an 'e': radios.

A space poem

Vocabulary work

1 a) inched b) stumbled / tripped
c) fall / rise d) 2 walk slowly

Note that 'plod' further suggests a heavy walk, walking with difficulty. Point out 'plod' is also used figuratively: James plodded through his homework.

e) steady

Point out 'steady' is also used as an adjective: The car went at a steady speed. / The candle burned with a steady flame. / My brother has a steady job.

f) lingered

2 a) a very bright light b) angry

3 strong

4 Example: John split the wood with his axe.

5 falls down

6 that it had been there for a very long time

Make sure students understand that 'ancient' is generally used of periods thousands of years ago. We speak of ancient Egypt, ancient Rome, ancient Greece – or say that Alexandria is an ancient city, and that the pyramids are ancient monuments.

7 arches (line 25)

Understanding

1 the first man on the Moon – Neil Armstrong

2 The speaker – he is here speaking to himself, to make himself concentrate on what he is doing.

3 Eagle is the name of a bird, but it is also the name of the lunar module.

4 'dead black sky' (line 17)

5 a) the dust settles slowly (line 24)
b) the jumps are 'lingering' (line 25)

6 dead (lines 15–18)

7 Example: I make long, slow, curving jumps.

8 a) How hot or cold it is.
b) a thermometer

9 How humid the air is – how much moisture it contains.

How the poem is written

1 no

2 The words are emphasised, and the slow deliberate movement of the astronaut is suggested.

3 Perhaps it gives the idea how the astronaut's mind is receiving new information, how he is trying to understand it all, a little at a time.

There are no certain answers to this and the previous question. The intention of the questions is to stimulate the students' imagination, and to draw their attention to the way the poet has attempted to convey both the astronaut's movement and how he was feeling and thinking.

4 Dead – used five times in lines 15–18.

Note that there is an interesting poem about space exploration, and another which compares reading to space travel, in Student's Book 1, Unit 5.

UNIT 5

When we are asleep

Part 1: A busy night!

Vocabulary work

Paragraph 1

1 a) remember
  b) memories
2 often / frequently
3 clear / strong

Ask what a vivid colour would be like – a bright colour. See also 'vividly' in Unit 3, page 29, line 1.

4 average (lines 3 and 4)

Paragraph 2

1 a) detect (line 6)
  b) signs (line 10)
  c) really (line 10)
  d) rapid (line 9)
2 a) decrease
  b) reduces (line 13)

Paragraph 3

1 often / frequently. (See paragraph 1, question 2, as 'rarely' and 'seldom' have the same meaning.)
2 plays
3 a) actors chosen for a play or film
  b) to show the word is used in a special way – we would not normally call people we dream about a 'cast'.

Ask why the writer uses this word – because he is comparing dreams to plays ('dramas' – line 18). Check if students know 'cast' as a verb meaning to throw: eg cast a rope, and the common and useful expressions: 'cast a look / glance / one's eye over something'.

4 necessary
5 incidents (line 15)

Understanding

Paragraph 1

A1 False – everyone dreams. (line 1)
2 True (line 1)
3 False – a hundred minutes is an average time, so some people dream more, and some less, and individuals dream different amounts on different nights. (lines 3–4)
4 False – these are average figures (lines 3–5). Note 'probably'. We cannot say dreams are *never* shorter than ten minutes.
5 False – again, average figures

Paragraph 2

6 False – the waves move more quickly. (line 8)
7 True (line 8)
8 False – 'signs of dreaming ... *in all mammals studied'* suggests there *could* be some mammals who have not yet been studied and may not dream. (line 11)
9 False – some birds dream. (line 12)
10 True (line 12)
11 False – they dream more. (lines 12–14)

Paragraph 3

12 False – 'dreams are *seldom* without people' means that sometimes (though rarely) they do not have people in them. (line 16)
13 True – two thirds (more than half, therefore 'most') are about people we know. (lines 17–18)
14 False – not *everyone*. Those blind from birth cannot see in dreams. (line 19)

15 False – smell is 'not so frequently' involved, which means smell may be involved, though not so often. (line 20)

B1 Add the numbers together and divide by five.

2 a) Because they cannot talk to us and tell us.

b) They can measure electrical waves in the brain; breathing; pulse rate; and they can observe eye movements.

3 a) the time when we dream

b) 'D' is the initial letter of 'dream'.

4 a) the beat of the heart

b) on the wrist or the neck

5 a) sight, sound, touch, smell and taste

b) all (though some more than others)

Part 2: Lucid dreaming

Vocabulary work

1 a) kind / sort

b) told / asked. (Note that 'ordered' would be too strong a word in this context.)

c) strange

2 Four – arms and legs are called limbs.

3 a) It could measure very small changes in electrical currents.

b) His/her feelings are easily hurt.

4 a) Each person was questioned alone – without the other person knowing what he/she said.

b) truly, exactly, without making any mistakes

Understanding

A1 False – 'not everyone ...' (line 24)

2 True (lines 26–27)

3 False – there are three things you cannot do: '... cannot turn round, ... look into a mirror, ... switch lights on and off'. (lines 47–49)

4 False – his arms and legs did not move, but there was movement in the muscles that the sensitive scientific instruments were able to detect. (line 32)

5 False – the passage does not tell us this. We are told that the researcher can give instructions to the dreamer *before* he goes to sleep, but not that he cannot communicate with the dreamer *while* he is asleep. (It would be hard to imagine how he could do this.)

6 False – they did not know one another. (line 37)

B1 Because he knew he had to send messages back to the scientist.

2 Because when they awoke, the dreamers remembered meeting one another in a certain place, and they could describe accurately what they had seen, said, and heard.

3 You cannot turn round, look in a mirror, switch lights on and off.

Part 3: What do dreams tell us?

Vocabulary work

1 'Ancient' is only used of periods of history, cities, or buildings which are very old. (See also the poem in Unit 4, last line.)

2 distant

Make sure students understand that 'distant' can refer to both space and time. However, 'recent' is used only to describe closeness of time. 'Near' describes closeness of distance.

3 feelings (line 62)

4 a) changed

b) want / wish for

c) permitted

d) worried

5 interpretation (line 53)

Check if students know what an interpreter is – a person who translates someone's speech into another language.

Understanding

1 a) We are told that the ancient Greeks believed people could be healed by telling their dreams to a doctor (paragraph 8). Nowadays people may also be cured by telling their dreams, eg to a pyschologist (paragraph 12).

b) We do not believe dreams can foretell the future. (paragraphs 8 and 9)

2 Because the people and events are altered.

3 People who are not allowed to dream become anxious and restless.

Paragraphing

paragraph 8: the third sentence. (The first two sentences tell us what the questions are, and the remaining sentences give the answers ancient civilisations proposed.)

paragraph 9: the second sentence. (The third and fourth sentences say what the feelings and events are. The first sentence, which also acts as a link to the first paragraph, says what we now do not believe dreams are.)

paragraphs 10, 11, 12: the first sentence of each paragraph

Dreams

Vocabulary / Understanding

1 wishes, desires, ambitions, aspirations

2 a) quick. (Note that 'quick' is an adjective: the adverb is 'quickly'.) Example: The mouse was too fast for the cat.

b) tightly / firmly. (Note that 'fast' here is an adverb – there is no word 'fastly'!)

Check if students know that we also use 'fast' to mean 'not easily moved': The truck was stuck fast in the sand. We also use it in the sense of a fast colour, which refers to a coloured fabric that will not fade with washing or in sunlight.

c) 'Fast' (verb) means not eating food, especially for religious reasons. The time or action of not eating is also called a 'fast' or 'fasting' (nouns).

3 Barren land is not fertile. It is unable to produce crops. A barren animal cannot produce young.

4 Lines 2 and 4 rhyme; lines 6 and 8 rhyme.

5 Line 5 is *exactly the same* as line 1; line 6 is *similar* to line 2.

6 a) a manner of speaking in which the qualities of a person or thing are described as being something else, something which it is like

b) A life without dreams is said to be a bird with a broken wing; a frozen field unable to produce crops.

You may decide to teach / remind students that a comparison using 'like' or 'as' is called a simile. So 'life is *like* a bird with a broken wing' would be a simile, not a metaphor.

Discussion

1 **Elicit that hopes and ambitions might be for bad things: a person might want to be a successful thief! Also, we might have an ambition to be something good and worthwhile, perhaps a doctor or a great sportsman, but we do not have the opportunity or ability. Failure to achieve such impossible ambitions may make us so disappointed that we fail to work hard to achieve what is possible and also worthwhile.**

2 **You might ask students to jot down say five ambitions each in note form. Go round the class. Write down the ambitions of the first student on the board. Ask the next student. Add any new ambitions – put a tick against any already on the board. When you have finished, you can see what are the most common ambitions – and which the most unusual. You could ask certain students to say more about their ambitions. This will give plenty of material for the writing assignment later.**

Spelling

musical	gentle	horizontal
vertical	obstacle	capital
single	shovel	horrible
animal	feeble	international
label	article	icicle
identical	vehicle	spectacle
comical	physical	terrible
towel	civil	mathematical
simple	hospital	uncle
vowel	quarrel	practical
apple	circle	model
tunnel	personal	paddle
candle	possible	probable

Make sure students understand the very important difference between the meanings of the last two words in the list: 'possible' – can / may happen; 'probable' – likely to be true: It is possible a meteor could destroy Paris, but it is not probable. (Check if students know what a meteor is – a piece of rock-like material travelling through space at very great speed.)

You might want to teach also the difference between counc*il* (noun) – a group of people, often running the affairs of a community; and couns*el* (noun and verb) meaning advice (noun) / to advise (verb) – note the difference in spelling. 'Advise' / 'advice' are used more often than 'counsel' in contemporary written and spoken English.

Punctuation

a) nap (line 1): a short sleep during the day

b) nightmare (line 7): a horrible dream, a horrible experience

c) snore (line 9): breathe in a noisy way while asleep

d) guillotine (line 15): a device for cutting off a person's head with a heavy falling blade

e) fan (line 18): an object, held folded, then spread out for moving air to cool the face

Explain that the French Revolution took place in 1789. Many rich people or those who did not support the revolution were executed. If students have used Student's Book 2 of this series, they may remember the story in Unit 6 of the Scarlet Pimpernel, set at the time of the French Revolution.

1C My uncle Charles once told me about the strange way a friend of his died. He had gone to the theatre to see a play. The play was set at the time of the French Revolution when many people were condemned to death by the guillotine.

2B My uncle's friend had been working hard all day. He was tired and fell asleep. He had this dreadful nightmare. He dreamt he himself was condemned to death. At this point he started to snore.

3D His wife tried to wake him, but(,) unfortunately(,) she tapped him lightly on the back of the neck with her fan. My uncle's friend died instantly of shock. His wife never went to the theatre again.

4A 'So if you ever see me taking a nap in my chair,' added my uncle, 'be a good boy(,) and just let me sleep. You wouldn't want to give me a shock, would you?'

1 His dream was based on the play he had just been watching.

2 a) The story could not be true because the friend did not wake up before he died. How could he have told his dream to the uncle?

b) The uncle wanted to be sure that when he had a nap, his nephew would leave him in peace.

UNIT 6

Reduce! Reuse! Recycle!

Changing the way we live

Pre-reading discussion

1 Petrol, diesel fuel, paraffin and heating oil are all refined (made) from crude oil (the oil that is pumped from the earth). We need these fuels for driving cars, flying aeroplanes, generating electricity, keeping warm and manufacturing. Modern civilisation depends on oil.

- Oil is found in many parts of the world, but much of it is a long distance from the industrialised countries. For example, most oil for European countries comes from Saudi Arabia and other countries in the Middle East.
- It has to be carried to Europe in supertankers. This is dangerous because a supertanker may sink or hit rocks, and so spill its oil. The oil can pollute the coastline for many miles. It can ruin the tourist industry and kill many fish, sea animals (such as seals) and seabirds. The feathers of birds become covered with oil, and they cannot fly.

2 Pollution means 'making dirty'. (Explain / elicit the verb is 'pollute'.)

3 Cars pollute with their exhaust fumes. Rubbish is usually buried or burnt on the outskirts of towns and cities. But space for burying rubbish is becoming more and more limited. Burning may pollute the atmosphere. Most plastic when buried does not rot away like wood and paper, and it cannot be destroyed by burning. (Some modern plastics do rot away if buried: they are called biodegradable.)

4 **Accept information, but do not give any at this stage – global warming is briefly described in paragraph 6 of the passage. Global warming is now a topic of great concern and is often dealt with in science textbooks for schools. It would be worthwhile finding out whether students have yet dealt with the topic there and what their textbooks have to say. It is possible you may be able to co-operate with the students' science teacher in this area.**

New vocabulary

It is no use crying over spilt milk: it is no use complaining / worrying about something after a misfortune has happened and when nothing can be done to put it right.

Vocabulary work

1 a) It is bigger. b) Something that is large.
c) 'Supermarket' is the most useful word.

Students may have seen films with Superman – a man with greater powers than normal men. Check if they know 'superior', eg a superior motor car is one that is better than most cars. You may choose to mention that 'super' is commonly used in very informal language to mean 'very good': We had a super holiday.

2 a) pull
b) a small ship that tows a larger one. Tugs regularly tow ships into or out of ports, particularly where the approach is dangerous or tricky. Tugs may also be used, as here, to pull shipwrecked ships off the rocks or shore.

3 a) A helicopter is a flying machine with a large rotor (like a fan) on the top.
b) A helicopter can hover (stay in the same place) in the air, and lower ropes, ladders, or rescuers to those in danger.

4 2 ready for when help, action, etc. is needed

5 b) that it covers a large area

6 a) in newspapers
b) They act as headings for news items and articles. They tell us briefly what they are about.

c) Supertanker hits rocks in *a* storm. Tugs and rescue helicopters *are* standing by. Thousands of tons of oil *have / are being* spilled into *the* sea. Extensive pollution of *the* coastline *is* predicted. (*The*) Clean-up costs could be millions.

Elicit that in headlines present tenses are used, even though the events have taken place in the past.

7 a) take hold of quickly and with force
b) make us take notice

8 merely (line 8)

9 hundreds of years ago

10 a) made

11 a) manufacture (line 19)
b) rapidly (line 17)
c) moreover (line 17) / in addition (line 20)
d) so (line 19)

Note that if 'consequently' is used, it must start a new sentence.

12 buses, vans, motorcycles, scooters (ie vehicles with engines – not pulled by animals)

13 a) 1 to stop or hinder a person's breathing
2 to cough and struggle for breath
b) block – the vehicles do not move, but their engines keep running and the streets become more full of fumes than if the vehicles were moving.

Explain that we also say that a drain is choked or blocked if water cannot run through it.

14 the gases which come out of vehicles

Explain further that the pipe the fumes come through is called the exhaust pipe or just 'the exhaust'. 'Exhaust' as a verb means to use up: After three days in the desert our supply of food was exhausted. It also means to make tired: We were exhausted after our long swim.

15 'Ocean' is used of larger areas of water.

Check if students know the names of the oceans and some seas of the world, eg the Atlantic Ocean, the Pacific Ocean, the Indian Ocean and the Mediterranean, the Black Sea, the Red Sea.

16 fumes (line 25) and gases (line 27)

17 a) round, like a ball
b) This refers to the world – a global problem is one that concerns everyone on earth.

18 e) weather

19 Pole – the North Pole and the South Pole

20 Example: covering many islands and low shorelines

21 'If we do not'

22 c) wanting too much of something

23 d) surroundings

24 d) people who live near you

Check that students know the other words, and in particular understand the difference between our 'ancestors' (who came before us) and our 'descendants' (who will come after us), and also that 'relatives' and 'relations' have the same meaning.

25 a) happily. (Ask how 'happily' can be made opposite in meaning by using a prefix – *un*happily.)
b) remember c) slowly d) high
e) big f) many g) much / a lot of
h) *dis*couraged i) fewer j) few
k) thick l) fall
m) increase. (Ask for the word of opposite meaning to 'increase' also ending in 'crease' – *de*crease.)
n) *im*possible (Note 'im-', not 'in-'.)
o) *ir*responsible p) *un*tidy

Students often have problems with the difference between 'much' and 'many' and 'few' and 'a few'. You might use the examples to explain the differences.

Understanding

A1 False – the writer says the pollution happens every few years (line 6), not 'all the time'. However, even if spillages were happening every day, that certainly would not mean they are unimportant – lines 1–5 make this clear.

2 True – newspapers (and of course TV) would not report shipwrecks if people were not interested in them.

3 False – paragraph 3 makes it clear that smoke polluted the atmosphere, and rubbish was thrown into rivers in the past, but only on a relatively small scale. It was therefore not a problem.

4 False – plastic causes pollution because most plastic cannot be destroyed (for example by burning), and so it has to be buried though it will not rot in the ground. In addition people just leave plastic items around to litter the environment.

5 True – when we use electricity, eg in the home, it does not cause pollution, but the electricity is produced in a generating / power station, which probably uses coal or oil.

6 True (lines 45–49)

7 True – 'that is the work of governments' (lines 44–45)

B1 The tugs will pull the supertanker off the rocks. The helicopters will rescue people.

2 millions of pounds or dollars – a great amount of money

3 Because every day we have fresh news of other great events in newspapers and on radio and TV. Also, if events are far away in the world, we think they do not affect us and so soon forget them.

4 Because we may forget how great the problem of pollution is, and so do nothing about it.

5 the growth of population – more people need power and transport and discard more rubbish; greater production of goods as we demand more things; an increase in the amount of plastic materials which cannot be destroyed

6 by advertising, especially on TV

7 Factories need power, which comes from power stations which burn coal or oil; manufacturing produces waste (eg chemicals) which may escape into the environment.

8 by oil spillages (first paragraph) and by poisoned waste being dumped into rivers and oceans (line 28)

9 the North and South Poles – mostly from the North Pole

10 a) italic – we can say that *now* is printed 'in italic' or 'in italics'

b) to emphasise / stress that the matter is urgent. We should act *immediately*.

11 a) The writer is giving information about pollution.

b) He/She is also trying to persuade us to do something about the problem.

12 The engines might have broken or someone might have made a mistake in navigating the boat (steering it).

Paragraph organisation

1 pollution

2 It is an exciting and frightening event which causes a great deal of damage. Similarly, we are more interested in an aircraft crashing and killing 100 people than learning that 100 people have been killed in road accidents or accidents in the home over a certain period.

3 pollution of the environment in the past

4 a) He introduces the first sentence with the words: 'But now ...'

b) the contrast between the situation now and in the past

5 air pollution from burning fuel such as oil or coal, or dumping waste into rivers and oceans

6 global warming because of destruction of the ozone layer

7 both individuals in their daily life and in their own neighbourhoods, and governments for large-scale pollution

Ask students what is meant by 'large-scale pollution' – pollution of whole cites, countries, oceans and the earth's atmosphere.

Spelling

a) rescue b) moreover c) roads
d) breathe e) exhaust f) daily
g) countless h) stations i) poisoned
j) oceans k) greatly
l) reuse ('Reuse' is the word in the passage, but 'raise'; and 'rouse' would also be correct.)
m) thoughtlessness n) individuals
o) neighbours

Mummy, Oh Mummy

New vocabulary

If appropriate for the level of the class, you may ask whether students know what other meanings 'pop' (line 23) has as noun and verb: (1) to describe the sound of a light explosion: There was a pop when we lit the gas ring. (2) to burst: Trevor popped the balloon. (3) to move quickly or for a short time: The mouse popped out of its hole. / I parked the car for just a few minutes to pop into the shop. / Margaret popped the letter into the box. (4) meaning 'popular' in expressions such as 'pop music'. (5) meaning 'father', but only in colloquial English (it is used more in America). Students should not use the word in this sense.

Vocabulary work

1 Daddy

Explain that shortened versions are 'Dad' and 'Mum' – these informal forms are generally used only within a family.

2 The word most probably means 'nation' here. The poem is set in the countryside, but here the mother includes factories and beaches and suggests everywhere is polluted. However, 'country' *could* have either or both meanings.

You might want to point out that in producing prose (non-poetry writing) we should try to be unambiguous and make it quite clear what we mean by a word, but in poetry, writers often deliberately use words that may have two or more meanings.

3 on a bed

4 containing food and drink

Explain that tin is a metal. Tins are made of steel with a very thin coating of tin.

5 a very small river

6 a row of bushes used as a fence / wall

7 foolish

Understanding

1 They are a mother and son or daughter. (Ask if we know whether it is a son or daughter – no.)

2 a) in the countryside – bushes (line 7), trees (line 16), the hedge (line 23), the wood (line 26) are referred to as being visible; fields (line 21) and streams (line 22) are also referred to, but not as visible objects
b) enjoying some time there – maybe having a picnic as pop bottles are mentioned (line 23)
c) home (lines 24 and 30)

3 a) four stanzas
b) eight lines in each stanza

4 the child (son or daughter)

5 pollution

6 What is pollution? Who makes it? Why don't they stop? What will happen if the pollution continues?

7 a) factories belching their fumes (line 5)
b) beaches covered with tar (line 6)
c) spraying crops (line 13)

8 a) dump a mattress
b) It is not likely they have brought the mattress with them on their day out, and she seems to be seeing the 'good place' for the first time.

9 a) throw sweet papers into the bushes (line 7) and throw two soft drink bottles over the hedge (line 23)

b) both littering the countryside with rubbish

c) so that she does not have the trouble of taking the items home

d) When the mother suggests throwing away the sweet papers (line 7), we may be surprised because she has just been saying that the country is 'in a mess' because of pollution. However, by the time she mentions getting rid of the bottles (line 23) we have already heard her suggesting dumping the mattress, too. She therefore seems to be the kind of person who feels that preventing pollution has nothing to do with her.

10 a) throwing away bottles and so polluting the wood

b) no

11 a) in the bath or in a washing-up bowl where the foam is made by soap

b) The foam would be made by chemicals polluting the water, not by waves as in the sea.

12 a) No – the poem is clearly telling us that pollution is wrong.

13 That every one of us should try to help reduce pollution – and that we should not encourage young children to pollute the environment. Parents should be a good example to their children.

You could refer back to the story in Unit 1, 'The fun they had', which was both humorous and serious. Stress that often the most effective poems and stories make serious points while also making us smile, just as jokes and amusing folk stories may have underlying morals or serious purposes. Can students suggest any such stories from their own culture?

14 'Selfish' is perhaps the best word: she thinks only of herself and her own convenience. She is also stupid in that she does not realise what she is doing.

Comparing the article and the poem

1 pollution from car exhaust fumes

2 the spraying of crops with insecticide / weed-killer (line 13). (Spraying crops to kill insects can of course be beneficial if used correctly – but the poem talks of harmless flowers which die because they are nearby. In addition insecticide may harm creatures who are not pests, or whose food source is killed by the sprays. Insecticides are carried by rainwater off the fields into streams and rivers where they may do more damage to wildlife.)

Rhyme

1 day / play, hope / soap, sun / run, real / feel

Elicit that words do not have to be spelt the same way in order to rhyme, eg hope / soap, real / feel, and that even if the ends of words are written the same, they may not rhyme, eg through / enough.

2 a) line 4 (without)

b) line 8 (car)

c) no line rhymes with line 5

3 stanza 2: bad / add (lines 10 and 12); bees / trees (lines 14 and 16)

stanza 3: on / gone (lines 18 and 20); foam / home (lines 22 and 24)

stanza 4: wood / good (lines 26–28); away / day (lines 30–32)

Ask which of these rhyming sounds are spelt differently – bad / add, on / gone, foam / home.

Discussion / Writing

Draw students' attention to how continuous paragraphs of speech or quotations by the same speaker are punctuated. The first paragraph starts with an opening quotation mark and if the quotation continues into other paragraphs, further quotation marks open each of these paragraphs, but a closing quotation mark is placed only at the very end.

Adela al Rouimi

A very courageous woman

Pre-reading discussion

You might like to ask the following questions, based on the photo on page 58, during the pre-reading discussion:

- The person in the wheelchair is about to throw something. Do you know what it is? (Elicit the object is a large metal ball. It is called a 'shot'. The competition is called 'putting the shot'.)
- What is the person in the white shirt doing? (Elicit that he is holding the wheelchair steady so the disabled athlete can put the shot.)

One way of approaching this interview would be to allocate each of these sections (1–18) to different members of the class (doubling up if necessary). Sections 2 and 3 are very short and could be put together. Ask students to look at their allocated section carefully, deciding how best to read *both* the interviewer's *and* Adela's lines to bring out the meaning and feeling, keeping in mind that questions should be asked like questions and not statements. It might be a good idea to allocate lines ahead of the lesson, so students can practise their section and read the whole interview. When you deal with the interview in class, you can first take all the parts of the interviewer. Students will in turn read Adela's replies. After subsequent discussion of the passage, repeat the reading, but reverse the roles so that you read Adela's lines.

Section 1 (lines 1–31)

Vocabulary work

1 promote (line 9)

2 a) a sort of hospital

Understanding

1 False –'We last met two years ago.' (lines 2–3)

2 Kuwait (line 21)

3 Switzerland (line 17)

4 She cannot walk. (line 22)

5 Kuwait – we learn later, in a radio studio. (line 131)

6 d) She tries to get back 'every six months' (lines 5–6); 'a few weeks' (line 14) refers to *this* visit (line 12), but we do not know whether this is the normal stay 'each time' as stated in (c).

7 False – she found it difficult in the beginning, then became self confident. (lines 27–31)

Section 2 (lines 32–89)

Vocabulary work

1 a school where you live for the whole of each term (between holidays)

2 The chief city of a country (where the governing body is): Cairo is the capital of Egypt; Amman is the capital of Jordan; London is the capital of the United Kingdom.

This can be made into a simple game to practise question and answer forms:

What is the capital of Japan? Tokyo.

Is Brussels the capital of France? No, it isn't. Brussels is the capital of Belgium. Paris is the capital of France, etc.

Note, many students will think New York (not Washington) is the capital of the United States.

3 a very young child

4 talk (with one another)

Understanding

1 False – the passage tells us she heard about the Stoke Mandeville games and wanted to take part in them. It does not tell us whether she ever took part in these games, nor does it say she went to the hospital for treatment.

2 Members had to use wheelchairs to get about.

3 False – we are told that this is a strange experience for them. (lines 71–73)

4 German speaking – she is fluent in German. (line 79)

5 Adela does not speak Arabic (lines 75–77 and lines 82–84) because she left Kuwait when she was only two years old (lines 19–20 and line 81), and her parents do not speak English. (lines 85–87)

***Additional question*: Ask students what the significance of 'really' is in line 56, and why 'is' has been printed in *italic* – the motto of the Olympic Games says that it is more important to take part than to win. The use of 'really' and italic indicates that Adela is stressing the point: that it is the taking part that 'really matters' in all sports competition. (Note there is useful information on the Olympic Games in Unit 2 of Student's Book 2. There is also a unit on Switzerland in Unit 4 of the same book.)**

Section 3 (lines 90–138)

Vocabulary

1 a) a heavy round object, like a plate, thrown in sports competitions

b) a stick with a sharp point (like a spear) thrown in sports competitions

2 chances

Understanding

1 Adela would have been in a wheelchair, so the girl would have known she was disabled.

2 advantages: an interesting job in publishing, her own apartment, opportunities for athletic training as a disabled person

disadvantages: being away from her family, not having servants, problems with snow

3 It is difficult to move a wheelchair through snow. (lines 127–128)

4 speaking with the interviewer

Reading aloud

If you have followed the earlier suggestions about reading the interview, the students should now be able to read more effectively in pairs. Tape recorders, if available, would be useful.

Paragraphing

The activities here are very important indeed, and care and time should be spent on them. They revise and reinforce essential skills in paragraph and text organisation which have been stressed in all three books of this course. The unscrambling exercises should not be too difficult for students at this stage, particularly if done as a group activity (ideally groups consisting of students of varying abilities).

You may decide to give help by giving the first sentence in each paragraph. Note that in this text the first sentence is always the topic sentence. This not only makes the exercise easier, but also reinforces the 'classic' form of the paragraph – the model which students should follow themselves when writing if they have problems in paragraph organisation. Though some help might be offered, it is much better for students to attempt to work out the ordering of both sentences and paragraphs for themselves as much as possible.

The sequencing of sentences within each paragraph is as follows:

paragraph A: 1, 3, 2

paragraph B: 3, 2, 1, 5, 4

paragraph C: 4, 3, 2, 1

paragraph D: 2, 1, 4, 3

paragraph E: 2, 3, 1

paragraph F : 2,1, 3

paragraph G: 1, 3, 2, 5, 4, 6

The order of paragraphs is:

1 – C 2 – B 3 – D 4 – G 5 – F 6 – E 7 – A

After students have unscrambled individual sentences and placed the paragraphs in order, they should write the piece out neatly themselves, maybe leaving a space between lines. This will reinforce their understanding of how paragraphs are organised and connected, as well as giving practice in neat handwriting and layout.

Students can now work on text cohesion (how ideas are bound together by conjunctions and connective phrases, introductory phrases, pronouns and the use of repetition). Go through the passage a paragraph at a time and discuss how these various devices have been used. Students can mark their versions *in pencil* (to make corrections easier) using different types of underlining (eg single / double straight lines, waved / dotted lines) as agreed with you. There are examples of all five connecting devices in the first paragraph. Work with the class on this paragraph, so they understand clearly what the five devices are. Students can then work, independently or in groups, on the rest of the passage, a paragraph at a time, subsequently checking / correcting their work with you as a class.

The following is the unscrambled version of text with connecting words, etc. marked as follows:

- Introductory words / phrases – underlined
- CONJUNCTIONS / SHORT CONNECTING PHRASES – CAPITALS
- ***Pronouns and the nouns they refer to – bold italic***
- Words repeated exactly – *italic*
- Words / expressions repeated in a different form – *(italic in brackets)*

C At one time ***the blind*** were generally considered unable to live a *normal* life. ***They*** might even be considered stupid, not fully human, and only to be *(pitied)*. BUT nowadays ***the blind***, like other *(disabled people)*, do not want *(pity)*. ***They*** just want a chance to live as *normal* a life as possible, both at work and play, and in their own homes.

B In the past, few *(types of employment)* were given to ***the blind***. Nearly all their *(jobs)* were hard and badly paid. FOR EXAMPLE, ***many of them*** *(wove baskets or carpets)*. ***A few*** became *(piano tuners)*. ***Fewer still*** became *(musicians)*, ***some of whom*** became very famous and rich.

D Now, ***blind people*** have more varied *(work opportunities)*. ***They*** can be found in many *(walks of life)*. ***Some*** have their own *(businesses)*. ***Others*** are *(professional people)* such as *(lawyers, professors, and teachers)*.

G One well-known example of a very successful *blind* person is the popular radio *presenter* *Peter White*. Some years ago the *BBC* had a regular *programme* about *blind* people. ***Peter White*** enjoyed the *programme*, but ***he*** wondered how a sighted *presenter*, however good, could really understand the problems of the *blind*. ***He*** told the ***BBC*** his views. SO ***they*** invited ***him*** to be the *presenter*. ***He*** NOT ONLY became very successful on that *programme*, BUT has since become a successful and popular *presenter* of other radio *programmes* AS WELL.

F BUT perhaps the best-known blind person today is our ***Minister for Education and Employment***. *(David Blunkett)* has to manage a huge government department, make speeches and answer questions in the House of Commons. YET ***he*** does not like the term *('handicap')* – ***he*** calls his *(blindness)* 'an inconvenience'.

E As for sport and recreation, it is truly amazing what ***many blind people*** have accomplished. ***They*** swim, become champion divers, canoeists and yachtsmen, and climb mountains. Perhaps even more remarkably, ***some*** *play golf*.

A To *play golf*, the blind *player* must have a sighted *helper*. The ***helper*** places the *ball* in the correct position at the start of play, and guides the *player* to each place the *ball* has been hit. ***He*** THEN advises on distance and direction to the hole, and the *player* has to judge just how hard and in what way to hit the *ball*.

Vocabulary extension

Describing sounds

1 a) ringing b) tinkling c) crashing
d) squeaking / creaking e) rumbling
f) rustling g) roar h) thud
i) scratching j) grating

2 a) a loud noise
b) shedding tears or crying when unhappy.

Stress that 'cry' is the more common word in this sense; 'weep' – past tense and past participle 'wept' – is commonly used in writing.

3 speaking in a hesitant way, often repeating a word or sound, as in: M-m-may I g-go h-h-home?

4 If you were in pain or complaining: 'More work to do!' groaned Paul.

5 a) angry
b) It makes a deep, angry noise and bares its teeth.

6 a) A chuckle is a little laugh, not very loud.
b) Giggling is a silly, childish way of laughing.

7 loud: screaming, shrieking, yelling;
soft: whispering, muttering, murmuring

8 a) by hitting both hands together
b) by hitting something or someone with the palm (flat) of the hand – giving a slap

9 No – if you moan, you are in either in pain, or you are complaining.

Note that 'moan' has a very similar meaning to 'groan'.

10 a) making a low continuous sound with closed lips
b) bees

11 a) a long high noise, especially indicating grief (very great unhappiness) or pain
b) perhaps someone has died.

12 a) birds, or large insects such as cicadas
b) dogs, foxes, wolves
c) lions
d) cats
e) donkeys, asses
f) birds
g) bees, or other small insects
h) cattle
i) dogs, lions. (A deep sound made when the animal is angry. We also say that people 'growl' if they are angry.)
j) snakes
k) mice
l) cocks
m) bulls. (We sometimes say a person bellows when speaking very loudly, perhaps when angry; note also 'bellow with laughter'.)

Smells

1 – c 2 – b 3 – a

Ask which of these three adjectives could be replaced by 'fragrant' – perfumed.

Touch

1 a) soft b) cold

Ask what 'warm' and 'cool' suggest – 'warm' is a lower temperature than 'hot'; 'cool' is between 'warm' and 'cold'.

c) rough d) sharp

2 sticky

Check if students know the verb 'stick' – to fasten things together, maybe with glue, or to fasten something, perhaps with a drawing pin, onto a wall or noticeboard.

3 a) very soft b) adjective c) sponge

Point out that the final 'e' of sponge is dropped to form 'spongy'. Check if they know what a sponge is. (1) a kind of simple sea animal that is soft and yellow, with a structure full holes, able to take in water easily; (2) a piece of this or something like it, used for washing, cleaning, etc.

4 something with a sharp point – a thorn, for example. (A spike is a piece of metal with a sharp point.)

Taste

1 a) something with sugar in it
b) old milk
c) something with salt in it
d) old bread / cake

2 That the food has a high temperature; it has in it chilli pepper or a similar spice which burns the mouth.

Note the adjective is 'spicy' – without an 'e'.

3 a) tasty

Point out that the final 'e' of 'taste' is dropped when making this adjective.

b) delicious

Spelling

1 a) apartment (line 120), independent (line 123), servant (line 121), important (line 135)

2 a) president b) accident c) inhabitant
d) immigrant e) confident (adjective)*
f) tolerant g) subsequent h) impudent
i) emigrant j) sergeant k) reluctant
l) pleasant m) sufficient n) abundant
o) elegant p) extravagant q) restaurant
r) frequent s) elephant t) urgent
u) transparent v) descendant
w) efficient x) patient y) excellent

* Note that there is a noun spelt 'confidant' – a friend you discuss things with – but students will not need to know / use this word at this stage.

3 current (noun) – flow of water, air, electricity, etc.: The current was too strong for the swimmer and he had to be rescued; (adjective) – present, happening at the moment: the current government / head teacher – the one now in power; current affairs – what is happening in the world at the moment

currant (noun) – a small dried grape, often used in cakes

Discussion

You may extend the discussion, if you think appropriate, to attitudes towards disability in the students' own community, and whether more might be done. Do they have any constructive proposals?

Writing

1 **You might like to discuss this question with all students, whether or not they decide to choose this as a writing topic because the answers to the essential points suggested revise what they remember of the passage, and also deciding what are the most interesting pieces of additional information should provoke discussion. Note that students are asked to look for the 'most interesting' pieces. The choice might be done individually, or on a group basis. Ask students to write down the three pieces of information each would include, then compare answers. Perhaps the two most likely suggestions are (1) Adela not speaking Arabic, and so having difficulties in communicating with her parents and (2) her difficulties in getting her wheelchair through snow. The point of the exercise, of course, is *not* getting 'correct' answers, but realising that there are often different but equally valid views when judging interest and relevance. Elicit that if the class went out on an outing together, and each member had on its return to write down the five most interesting things seen, the lists might be very different.**

UNIT 8

The restless planet

A close look

Pre-reading discussion

Accept any information students may offer about earthquakes, and prompt them as appropriate into describing what happens in an earthquake. Do not give further information – the passage will provide more. Ask them to explain the title. Elicit that a planet is one of the large objects that move round the sun. Earth is one of these planets. 'Restless' means not able to stay still. We often use 'restless' of a person, eg of someone who cannot settle in one place or job. Here in the title, however, it refers to earthquakes.

Vocabulary work

Paragraph 1

1 When he/she is frightened. (If he/she is cold we usually use the word 'shiver'.)

2 a) rigid (line 5)

Explain that these words are also used for attitudes and rules: a rigid / inflexible rule would have no exceptions; a flexible timetable could adapt to circumstances.

b) natural (line 3)

c) surface (line 4)

d) slowly (line 5)

3 d) opposite meanings

Give some examples of use: We squeezed the lemons. / The whole family squeezed into our small car. / My uncle's income will not stretch to a new car. Note also the useful phrasal verb 'stretch out': The road stretched out for miles. / We stretched out on the beach in the sun.

4 happen

Paragraph 2

5 a) most

b) especially

c) falling

d) destroyed

e) died

6 a) vulnerable (line 20)

b) energy (line 17)

c) built (line 20)

d) estimated (line 30)

Paragraph 3

7 a) great, important

b) minor

8 a) moving from side to side or backwards and forwards

b) I swayed on the deck as the ship was hit by strong waves.

Ask students to suggest a word that could replace 'sway' – rock.

9 a very tall building

10 a floor

Draw attention to the spelling: storey / storeys – not to be confused with story / stories.

Paragraph 4

11 beneath the (bottom of the) ocean / sea

12 a) harmful

Remind students that '-ful' not '-full' is the suffix, eg beautiful.

b) Too much exposure to the sun can be harmful.

13 a) adjective

b) tide. (Elicit what tides are – the rise and fall of the sea about every twelve hours.)

14 deep

15 sloping

16 very large, immense

17 a wide area

Paragraph 5

18 a) people in an early stage of development

Note the question asks 'which *best* describes ...' – primitive people may or may not have been warlike (b) and of course 'advanced' societies are also warlike. Primitive people were certainly not foolish (c) – they may not have understood science and had beliefs different from modern man, but they successfully hunted, fished, made things and lived in communities. People who lived a long time ago (d) were often relatively advanced in many ways, eg the ancient Egyptians. Elicit suggestions – they invented a form of writing, they built pyramids, they knew a great deal about the stars, etc.

19 A very large person, especially in old stories – where giants are much larger than would be possible in real life.

Point out that 'giant' is often used as an adjective meaning 'very large': A giant rocket took the spacecraft into space. 'Gigantic' is another adjective made from 'giant'.

Understanding

1 a) False – 'a skyscraper *may* be the safest place to be' – you cannot be *sure*. (lines 34–36)

b) False – 'cities are very vulnerable ... collapsing buildings ... fires ...' (lines 19–23)

c) True (paragraph 1)

d) False – this was a primitive belief – but 'primitive people did not understand how earthquakes were caused'. (lines 52–53)

e) True – 'the vast majority are small and cause little or no damage' (lines 15–16)

f) False – the article says nothing about this, but says that skyscrapers sway like trees. (lines 40–42)

2 Because the energy is created when rocks move against one another deep underground. An atomic bomb would explode on the surface.

3 the first atomic bomb (line 19)

4 Because buildings collapse and fires start. (lines 21–23)

5 Because the earthquake happened when many cooking stoves were lit. (lines 26–27)

6 'Common sense' would suggest that a tall building would be more dangerous and more likely to fall over.

This is a good opportunity to be sure the students know the useful phrase 'common sense' – practical good sense.

Paragraph organisation

The first sentence of each paragraph is a topic sentence.

This article is in fact very well organised. The information in each paragraph illustrates and expands on the opening topic sentence. It is well worth going over the article in detail with students, studying how this is done.

Pronouns

a) the rock plates (line 5)

b) the breaking and moving of the rock (lines 8–9)

c) cities (line 19)

d) most earthquakes (line 43)

e) waves (line 46)

An earthquake destroys El Asnam

Vocabulary work

Paragraphs 1 and 2

1 a) rubble (line 6)
b) massive (line 15)

2 a) hastily (line 23)
b) immediately (line 21)
c) prepare (line 38)
d) told (line 36)
e) erected (line 24)

Ask what else mentioned in paragraph 2 would be 'erected' – the tents.

3 a group of people bringing help from different countries

4 a) a light
b) The messages were sent very quickly.

Point out that 'in a flash' is a common expression meaning 'very quickly' or 'immediately': Roger is very good at science. He understands new ideas in a flash.

5 emergency (line 21)

Point out that this is a definition of the noun. Often, as in the passage, 'emergency' is used as an adjective, eg an emergency exit out of a restaurant or cinema would be used if there was a fire. An emergency operation in a hospital is one that must be carried out immediately.

6 a place where soldiers live

7 They made it difficult for lorries to bring help.

Paragraphs 3, 4, and 5

8 You press hard on it, destroying it.

9 a) all the time
b) very / extremely tired
c) very / extremely happy

Paragraphs 6 and 7

10 walking slowly, in a leisurely manner

11 a powerful tractor for moving earth and rubble

12 a low deep sound you make when you are in pain

13 a broad flat piece of concrete

14 He was taken out with care.

Understanding

1 a) True – there had been one in 1954. (line 9)
b) False – the earthquake broke the instruments *after* measuring it. (lines 17–19)
c) False – rescue operations started immediately. (lines 20–21)
d) False – they survived *mainly* (not *only*) on lemonade. (lines 62–64)

2 a) They put out fires.
b) They help remove survivors from crashed vehicles.

3 Because the older buildings had been destroyed in the previous earthquake.

4 The line between two of the rock plates that cover the surface of the earth.

5 Powerful lights used outside to light up an area. Floodlights are used at many football stadiums.

6 a) for people to live in
b) to keep them warm
c) Water would have been contaminated / polluted when the pipes were broken and these tablets would make it safe to drink.
d) for blood transfusions for injured people

7 Specially trained dogs can smell human beings buried under the rubble.

8 When he was trapped under the collapsing shopping centre (lines 72–74), he could have been hit by falling masonry (concrete or bricks) or completely buried.

Although he was trapped in a 'small space' (line 75) without food or water for a long time, he was lucky to have air.

A bulldozer could have disturbed the rubble or accidentally pushed him further into the collapsed building. (lines 81–82)

If the drivers had not stopped for coffee (lines 82–84) and switched off the machines, one of them would not have not heard him groaning. (line 85)

A further tremor (line 91) could have disturbed the concrete slab.

The rescuers might have caused rubble or slabs of stone or concrete to fall on him in the eight hours it took to dig him out. (lines 93–94)

9 If the driver had not gone for the coffee, he would not have stopped his bulldozer and later on heard the groaning.

10 Because the material that trapped him had to be removed very slowly and carefully. Otherwise it might easily have collapsed and buried him completely.

11 c) they were very anxious about what was happening

Invite / give some more examples, eg Two runners seemed to have broken the tape at the same time. / We held our breath as we waited for the result to be decided by the judges.

12 Good – otherwise it would have fallen on him.

13 Because Mohamed Sabi was an elderly man.

Paragraphing

1 a) 3 To give information about the 1980 earthquake, etc.

Explain how the other suggestions support this one main idea.

b) the fifth sentence: 'The 1980 earthquake ... the new town.' (lines 14–16)

2 the first sentence

3 e) Heavy casualties in the city.

Explain how the rest give support to this main idea.

4 the rescue of a two-month-old baby

5 a) the number of casualties; the rescue of six people

b) after the first sentence

c) Although it is dealt with in only one sentence, the first topic is the more important because it illustrates the extent of the tragedy. The second topic takes up more lines and is perhaps more memorable because of how people survived partly on the lemonade. It has high 'human interest' value, but is clearly less important to the topic of the whole article – the great damage and casualties caused by this earthquake.

6 Paragraph 6 tells how Mohamed Sabi was trapped. Paragraph 7 tells how he was found and released.

Spelling

reliable	possible
visible	capable
agreeable	flexible
probable	fashionable
comfortable	incredible
avoidable	noticeable
horrible	valuable
sensible	edible
responsible	miserable
lovable	indescribable

UNIT 9

The wooden horse

Pre-reading discussion

1 Elicit / teach meaning of the verb 'kidnap' – to capture and imprison someone illegally, demanding money (a ransom) with threats of violence, etc. – and the noun 'kidnappers' (line 6).

2 cutting through bars / making holes in walls / climbing over walls / digging a tunnel / making copies of keys / bribing guards / using disguise / hiding in something that is taken out of the prison

Before reading the story, ask if students know when the Second World War (see line 1) took place – 1939–45 – and who the countries involved were – the Allied Powers (principally Great Britain, France, the United States and the USSR) versus the Axis Powers (principally Germany, Italy, and Japan).

The following information can be given to students either before or after they read the story – the latter is recommended.

This unit recounts a true story. It was first told in a book, then a film, called *The Wooden Horse*. The wooden box used in gymnastics for vaulting is called a 'horse' and this appears in the story. The title of the book and film refers also to a well-known Greek legend about a much larger wooden horse. The legend, which is told in Homer's *Iliad*, says that armies from Greece besieged the city of Troy, in Asia Minor, for many years, without success. They could not break down the walls of the city. Then the Greeks had the brilliant idea of building a huge wooden horse inside which men could hide. One night they left the horse outside the main gate of the city. The next morning the Trojans found the horse and examined it carefully, but could not decide what it was or how it had come there. They decided to bring it into the city and examine it further. The following night secret trapdoors in the horse were opened and a group of Greek soldiers crept out of it. They attacked the guards at the city gates, opened the gates and let more Greek soldiers in. In this way, the city was captured.

Invite students to suggest similarities and differences between the Greek legend and this real modern escape story. Here men are escaping from a camp, not entering into a city, and the 'horse' is a small vaulting horse, not a huge wooden statue.

If students have ready access to reference material, you can ask them to research the wooden horse of Troy for themselves, and then share information in class. Fuller accounts can be found in most encyclopaedias - search: *Troy, Trojan War, Homer,* and *Iliad.*

Part 1

Diagram, page 75: Be sure students understand the plan of the camp. Ask:

- What are the nine large rectangles in the centre? (huts)
- Which is the barbed wire fence? (the double line)
- How many watchtowers are there? (seven)
- What do you think the large single-line rectangle inside the high fence shows? The answer – a low wire marking the furthest point to which prisoners might go to the fence – is not in the text and students must make a sensible guess. If prisoners crossed it, they might be shot by guards in the watchtower – see Student's Book, page 82.
- What do you think the vertical double line (like a path) might be at the bottom? We are not told, but there are clues in the text. (A tunnel / tunnelling is mentioned in lines 11 and 20.)

Drawing, page 76: Ask what the horizontal bar is for – carrying the horse. Elicit that though the drawing shows just one bar, another would slide through the horse at the other end. When the horse was being stored in a hut or in use, the bars could be removed.

Vocabulary work

Paragraph 1

1 a) daring (line 2)
  b) tried (line 1)

Paragraph 2

2 b) encircled

3 a) sentry

b) A sentry is a soldier who guards people or places.

Point out that sentries are always *soldiers*. A guard at a bank would be called a security guard, not a sentry.

4 a) a brush

b) The searchlights are constantly moving from side to side across the camp like a brush.

5 They move regularly around the area they are protecting, looking for problems.

6 Stilts are long wooden poles. They may be used to support a house especially when it is liable to be flooded. The word is also used for the poles with footrests used by people (often entertainers) for walking high off the ground.

7 a) They were of different colours.

b) showing a difference, easily seen and noticed among others: Policemen wear distinctive uniforms. / He spoke English with a distinctive Australian accent.

8 a slight shaking or trembling movement: The ground vibrates in an earthquake. / A machine may vibrate if it is not running smoothly.

9 a) The instruments record even the slightest vibration.

b) The person's feelings are easily hurt; he/she is easily upset.

Note another use of this very useful adjective: a sensitive skin (affected by sun or chemicals in soap, etc.).

10 b) being kept alone

Note the nouns 'solitude' – a state of being on your own – and 'solo' – alone: The pilot flew solo across the Pacific. Louise sang a solo in the concert.

11 a) prevent (line 11)

b) detect (line 17)

Ask what word describing a type of policeman is made from 'detect' – detective.

Paragraphs 3-6

12 a) jump over something, using hands for support

b) a box you jump over

13 It will no doubt stop you thinking about escaping. / No doubt, it will stop you thinking about escaping. / It no doubt will stop you thinking about escaping. (The first sentence is the most 'natural' order. In the other two sentences, the less natural placing of 'no doubt' means it is being emphasised.)

14 a number of people, vehicles, etc. following each other in order

15 a) fit (line 27)

b) clumsy (line 46)

16 deep

17 He became discouraged. / He no longer felt he was able to jump.

You might take the opportunity of teaching other English expressions with 'heart', eg 'good hearted' – kind; 'to break someone's heart' – make very sad: It broke my uncle's heart to leave his country; 'learn by heart' – memorise; 'heartless' – cruel; 'eat heartily'; 'hearty laughter'; 'hearty welcome'.

Understanding

1 Because you might be shot by the guards. (Note that the question uses 'dangerous', not 'difficult'.)

2 So that prisoners could not start tunnelling from them.

3 Yes, he believed this would keep the men fit, and stop them thinking about escaping – the exercise would take up all their thoughts and energy, and they would be too tired.

4 He probably pulled the horse over deliberately so that the guards could see clearly that this was just an empty box, that there was nothing suspicious in it. (The passage does not state this explicitly, but ask students what *suggests* this, ie Why else

would the writer mention this incident? Why does the writer use 'seemed' in line 48? Is this a clue that the jumper was only pretending?)

Paragraphing

1 The last sentence. This gives the topic of the whole story: this particular escape. The others give background information about it.

2 The first sentence. The others illustrate *how* and *why* escape seemed impossible.

3 It tells us that one prisoner had a brilliant idea. The third paragraph tells us what this idea was.

4 The first sentence in each paragraph

paragraph 4: The first sentence tells us how the box was brought out – the next two sentences tell us *what* happened then; how it was inspected by guards and used by the prisoners.

paragraph 5: The first sentence states there was an accident. The other sentences give us *more information* about it and say *what happened because* of it.

paragraph 6: The first sentence introduces the 'terrible jumper' – the other sentences tell us *how* he was a poor jumper, and *what* he did.

Part 2

***First drawing*: Elicit how it is now clear why the horizontal bars were essential: they not only made carrying convenient, but with men and sandbags inside, the weight of the horse would make them essential.**

Vocabulary work

1 a) enthusiastic

b) Example: James is not very enthusiastic about coming with us to the cinema. He says he has seen the film. / Katharine is very enthusiastic about going to Paris. She loves travel.

2 b) lessened

3 horizontal

4 a) 4 A long narrow passage … building.

Discuss how this meaning differs from the one in the passage – this shaft is not in a mine or a building. Elicit that dictionaries cannot give every possible meaning exactly, but this is clearly the closest meaning.

b) They all describe something long and narrow.

5 'Sprinkle' means to throw something around in small drops or pieces: We might sprinkle sugar on fruit. / We might sprinkle salt and pepper on meat.

Understanding

1 a) no

Check that students understand just why the men needed the sandpit. It was essential to place the box *exactly* in the same place each day, so that it was *exactly* over the trap door. Having the sandpit helped the men know where this place was and gave a reason for always putting the box in the same spot that would not make the guards suspicious.

b) He did it to show there was nothing suspicious inside it, or beneath it. (See also answer to Part 1, Understanding, question 4.)

2 If the tops of the wooden sides were too close to the surface, a guard might have felt it with his probe.

3 The thin wooden sides would have sunk deeper into the ground.

4 because the smaller the shaft the better

Ask why it needed to be small – (1) less digging was needed to make it; (2) less sand would have to be removed; (3) smaller pieces of wood were needed for the sides and fewer bricks for the foundation. Wood and bricks must have been hard to find in the camp. Also, wood and bricks had to be carried out.

5 So that the digger could turn round and start digging.

6 a) The top sand was grey.

b) The sand the digger was removing was yellow. If he placed yellow sand on the top, the guards would know someone had been digging.

7 They were hung from hooks inside the top of the box.

8 First of all, the bags of sand for removal from the site were hung on the hooks in the box. Then the trapdoor was replaced. The sandbags were put on top of the trapdoor. Finally, grey sand was sprinkled over the sandbags.

9 Because there was not enough room inside the box and the bags were heavy.

Paragraphing

1 the first sentence

2 The first time a man was taken out / carried out.

3 How was the vertical shaft made?

4 Why was progress very slow?

Part 3

Vocabulary work

Paragraph 11

1 a) about (line 92) b) quicker (line 91)

c) system (line 94)

d) reinforcement (line 91)

e) complete (line 89) f) devised (line 94)

Explain that 'devise' is regularly used of a plan, method, or way of doing something.

Paragraph 12

2 a) stayed (line 95)

b) shift (line 98)

3 'Drag' suggests pulling something with difficulty. (Mention that a person who is tired 'drags himself along'.)

Paragraph 13

4 The roof and / or walls fall down.

5 The man succeeded in digging himself free.

Check if students understand the need to change the particle: 'manage *to*', but 'succeed *in*'.

6 b) probable

7 a) A compass shows you the direction you are going in: a magnet swings round to the magnetic north pole.

Note that the drawing instrument used for making a circle is called 'a pair of compasses'.

b) A spirit level is a tool which shows if something is flat / horizontal. It consists of a bubble, which has to be centred within a small container of oil. It ensured the men did not dig upwards to the surface too soon or too deeply into the ground.

8 a) The men had made the instruments themselves.

Point out that 'home made' can suggest that something is good, or not very good. A home-made cake would suggest one better than could normally be bought in a shop. But here it suggests something that might not be accurate because making such instruments needs the correct tools and skill.

9 carefully

10 a) Something long and thin that could be pushed through the earth. A poker is long, thin, made of metal and used for stirring the wood or coal on a fire to make it burn better.

b) push into, out of, or through: Peter poked his head out of the window.

Understanding

1 This part was close to the vaulting horse. The men would be running up to it and jumping over it, thus causing a lot of vibration.

2 b) Less – with one man, twelve bags a day were removed (lines 86-88); with two men, nine bags a day *on average* (36 divided by 4 days).

Ask if the man in the box would do any digging on the three 'removal' days – no, because the tunnel was now too long, and in any case there would be no room in the box for more than twelve bags.

3 a) yellow

b) The sand on the surface was grey, but the sand underneath was yellow. If guards saw yellow sand, they would know that men had been digging.

4 People do not normally want to get wet.

Check if students understand 'suspicious' / 'suspicion' – a feeling of doubt, a feeling that something is wrong – and can use the words. Examples: The customs officer was suspicious of the bag, which was small, yet very heavy. / I have a suspicion that Tony is not really working hard for his examinations.

5 Because the diggers needed to be warned, and they needed time to rearrange the trapdoor and sandbags.

Ask how the men jumping could signal to the men digging – they would have to tap on the box when the guards were not looking. Ask how the diggers could contact the jumpers – a man would have to be near the box all the time to listen. Elicit how he would avoid making the guards suspicious – he might be helping jumpers over, or catching them if they fell. He would have to listen very hard because of the noise from the jumpers.

6 To see how long the tunnel was / whether the diggers had passed the fence.

Paragraphing

1 Starting work on the tunnel itself (rather than the shaft).

2 A system / way / method of digging with two men.

3 The last sentence of paragraph 11 tells us the topic of the next paragraph – 'a new system'.

4 a) the first sentence

b) They explain what the problems are.

Part 4

Vocabulary work

1 a) outside

b) most

c) minimum

2 a) conceal (line 122)

b) 1 tense (line 124)
2 fortunately (line 126)

c) eventually (line 132)

3 a) false documents – such as identity cards or passports. (Explain if necessary 'forge' means to copy in order to deceive – such as money or a signature.)

b) A country which is not involved in a war, which supports neither side.

4 bravery

Elicit / teach the adjectives formed from 'courage' and 'bravery' – 'courageous' and 'brave'.

Understanding

1 The sandbags had to be placed over the trapdoor and then *grey* sand sprinkled over the top.

Check if students remember why it had to be grey sand – the sand on the surface was grey, the sand below was yellow. (lines 14–15)

2 a) If they had worn their civilian clothes in the tunnel, they would have become dirty from the soil.

b) These black clothes made them harder to see in the dark – remember the searchlights and watchtowers.

3 As the escapers dug the last few metres of the tunnel, they had to place the soil they dug out behind them. This sealed the tunnel. There was a limited amount of air in the tunnel. If they used up all the oxygen before they broke out, they would have suffocated / died from lack of air.

4 They could not be easily seen from a watchtower as they broke out. Searchlights swept the camp (Part 1, paragraph 2). They could wait hidden in the ditch for the best time to get out and run.

5 They had a long way to go to reach safety. They had to reach and cross Denmark (then occupied by Germany), then cross the sea to Sweden. (A map would be useful for students here.) Only one of them spoke good German. They had badly forged papers. They would need food and shelter. They would probably have to find a railway and goods trains to hide in to travel a long distance.

Diagram, page 84: Ask if it shows the very last or penultimate (next to last) time the horse was taken out – the very last: one escaper is already waiting, the man in the middle will replace the trapdoor and sandbags, then return in the horse.

Paragraphing

1 The second sentence because this paragraph is about the new problem. The first sentence tells us *when* this problem occurred. Sentences 3 and 4 explain *what* the problem was. The last sentence states the *solution* to the problem.

2 a) The second paragraph would start 'Then on the next ...'. (line 120)

b) Because the two paragraphs have a similar theme – they are both about the escape, and the second paragraph would be very short. (Stress that both ways are correct. A piece of writing can often be divided into paragraphs in more than one way.)

3 How the escapers finally dug themselves out.

4 How the escapers returned to England.

Spelling

Part 1

a) daring, prevent, yellow, sensitive, instruments, digging, tunnelling, attempts, brilliant, activity, procession, padded, accident, finally

b) thousands, impossible, surrounded, guards, buried, solitary confinement, obviously, vault, doctor, terrible, laughed

Part 2

a) heavier, friends, pieces, their

b) regular, commander, prisoner, metre*, similar

*** metre – compare 'meter': an instrument for measuring something passing through it, such as electricity or water; also American English spelling of 'metre'**

Note that none of these words end '-or' as suggested, though this is a common ending, and would be pronounced the same. Invite students to suggest words: (1) describing people – actor, solicitor, inspector, governor, author, conjuror, editor, emperor, professor, spectator, doctor (occurs in line 44); (2) describing things – mirror, tractor, meteor.

Part 3

Corrected words: quicker, reinforcement, likely, compass, cautiously, fortunately

Part 4

Corrected words: fence, journeys, calculations, beginning, poorly, resourcefulness